W9-CAY-877

THE ASSOCIATED PRESS
GUIDE TO

NEWS
WRITING

Rene J. Cappon

Prentice Hall
New York • London • Toronto • Sydney • Tokyo • Singapore

Second Edition

Prentice Hall General Reference
15 Columbus Circle
New York, NY 10023

An Arco Book

Arco, Prentice Hall, and colophons are
registered trademarks of Simon & Schuster, Inc.

Manufactured in the United States of America

2   3   4   5   6   7   8   9   10

Library of Congress Cataloging-in-Publication Data

Cappon, René J. (René Jacques), 1924-
    The Associated Press guide to news writing / René J. Cappon—
2nd ed.
    p. cm.
Revised ed. of: The word.
ISBN 0-13-053679-2
1. Journalism—Authorship. I. Cappon, René J. (René Jacques),
1924- Word. II. Associated Press. III. Title.
PN4783.C283   1991   91-14041
808'.06607—dc20   CIP

Contents

Foreword

This book is aimed at a select audience: those who care about precise and attractive use of the language.

If you are in that company, read on. For here you will find—in a mix of humor, common sense and only occasional editorial pique—a guide to help you achieve what should be every journalist's aim, telling the reader what you mean in a crisp and correct way.

Perhaps the problem is the speed with which daily journalists must do some of their work. Perhaps it is that sameness of some of what we write—today's baseball game being normally not very different from yesterday's, this week's council meeting straying into predictable clichés, today's news briefing advancing us little if at all toward better understanding of the subject.

Whatever the reasons, the problems that persist in everyday news writing are not hard to identify and it is to these that this manual speaks.

We talk here not of an idyllic newsroom where the final four-paragraph accounts of auto accidents can be the leisurely product of a third and fourth rewrite. No, we deal here with what the careful writer (and editor) can do in a busy newsroom to bring to news copy the clarity and the appeal it must have at a time when so many other activities beckon for the reader's attention.

So, good writing is a practical matter; the story must be well written if it is to be well read.

But more tellingly, it is a professional matter. We should feel pride in doing our jobs well and in fulfilling our obligation to serve the reader well.

In the tumult of the last decade, as journalists have found themselves caught in unaccustomed legal and professional controversy, thousands of speeches have been given in defense of what we call "the people's right to know."

Let us also recognize the people's right to understand and be entertained. In support of these comes this guide for the careful use of our most precious asset—the word.

LOUIS D. BOCCARDI
President and General Manager
The Associated Press

About the Author

From a writer's point of view, the best circumstance is to have Jack Cappon, in the flesh, as your editor. Next best is to have at hand, for consultation or merely occasional picnicking, a collection of his ideas on the use of the language.

This book provides such a larder. What it does not provide are the gurgles and the sighs and the groans that rise from behind his desk when he comes upon sentences that are particularly well turned or upon writing that is lazy or pompous or dull. What makes Jack Cappon an editor, and not just a blue penciler with an academic interest in syntax, is that his romance with the English language is visceral. When people who should know better abuse the language, Jack Cappon hurts.

You will catch the flavor of Cappon in the flesh as you meander through Cappon in print. In his chapter on quotes, for example, he refers to stock bromides that "have the appeal of bovine cud." In his discussion of overloaded leads, he cites an especially turgid one about a ballet performer and remarks, "It's a wonder the writer neglected to add the first nine bars from *Swan Lake*." Vintage Cappon. Those are the sorts of comments AP writers routinely find scribbled in the margins when he sends back their copy for reworking.

The name on his birth certificate, issued in Vienna in 1924, is Rene Jacques Cappon. (One preachment of this book is to prefer the plain word to the fancy one; "Jack" will do.) He grew up speaking German, which he still does, and Hungarian, which he has forgotten. English he started at school in Vienna, along with Latin and Greek, which he pursued in high school in New York but reluctantly dropped at the University of Iowa.

Of all those languages, English was the one that seduced him. In conversation with habitués of the AP Newsfeatures Department, the "Poets' Corner" over which Cappon presided, he often mused aloud about the mystery of the language, the magic that makes certain combinations of words fit together, like notes in a musical score, while the same words in other combinations jar. He never tires of discussions of this sort.

Cappon served as AP Newsfeatures editor from 1958 to 1962, after toiling in AP bureaus in Baltimore, Frankfurt and Kansas

City. Later he became AP Managing Editor. As General News Editor, he again took over stewardship of the Poets' Corner in 1977.

Jack asked me to serve as editor of this book. The pleasure was mine, though the role reversal a bit strange. (Who will oversee the overseers?) He has chosen to cite as examples in his text a sentence or two of my origin. The eye and the ear and that chimerical thing in Jack Cappon called taste have improved the writer of those lines. Over the years, he has enhanced us all.

JULES LOH
Special Correspondent
The Associated Press

Author's Note

Any word book like this guide is, in a sense, a collaboration. My collaborators have been numerous; I count among them the people on the staffs of The Associated Press and AP member newspapers who have been subjected to writing workshops I have given over the years. Rather than a systematic journalism manual, the book is extended shoptalk—a continuation of the discussions, formal and informal, with news writers intent on improving themselves in their craft.

Much news writing is, of course, done under deadline pressure, and it isn't always possible to hone and polish. But, too often, time limitations are invoked as an excuse for the kind of carelessness that springs more from poor writing habits than any other cause. Writers who trouble themselves about technique can adjust to these rush hours without turning slipshod.

Certain questions kept recurring at the workshops: How do I enliven my style? What's true color? How do I avoid limp leads without teetering into hysterical ones? What makes for good feature writing?

Much of the AP guide is devoted to such practical matters. I have tried to show what works, what doesn't, and why, as much by examples from copy as by commentary. These snippets of instructive prose stem mostly from the AP report, which was naturally handiest for me, with others from newspapers around the country.

I owe a debt to these largely anonymous contributors, triumphant or limping in the heat of the daily battle.

I also owe specific debts. I am especially grateful to AP Special Correspondent Jules Loh, who edited *The Associated Press Guide to News Writing* with gentle wisdom. I owe thanks, too, to Executive Editor (now AP President) Lou Boccardi, who read the manuscript and offered valuable suggestions and criticism.

For errors that have slipped through this fine screening, I bear sole responsibility. I suppose that some will be found; a corollary to Murphy's Law states that anyone who writes a book on writing will inevitably commit some of the gaffes he warns against. Some readers no doubt will find certain judgments of mine open to question—as too dogmatic, too lenient, or altogether wrongheaded. Perhaps so. What matters more to me is the hope that this work might stir some writers, new and old, to think more about the process of writing, to remember that the first duty of language is to communicate, and that words can be the best of friends or the worst of enemies.

R. J. C.
New York, 1991

LANGUAGE: Pompous, Pedantic and Plain

1

News writing should be clear, concise, accurate and interesting. No one dissents from that proposition. But news is perishable, deadlines glare, resources are finite, big stories break unannounced—the pulse of daily journalism keeps racing. How much can you expect under such conditions?

But granting a measure of endemic disorder in the news business, it's also true that much excellent copy is being written daily. And a far more curious fact emerges from a study of news writing in many places: Stories written at relative ease show much the same flaws as those written under pressure.

That clearly suggests that something outside of the newsroom process is at work. There can't be many reporters who don't know, in their hearts, that they should keep things simple and direct and strip clutter from their prose. Yet at the keyboard, amnesia sets it.

"To write well is as difficult as being good," said Somerset Maugham. There may be a connection. To be good takes a high level of moral awareness. To write well takes a high level of technical awareness. We usually lapse from inattention, not ignorance. We fudge the small, measured steps, the care for details, that craftsmanship demands.

And so it happens that a portion of the news report is like a river in flood, sweeping along a great many things that shouldn't be there: trees, drowned raccoons, front porches, old shoes. The sight can be heartrending.

Start with such tiny clutter as the "up" in "free up" or "head up." Contemplate "ongoing" or "currently," as in "he is currently the president of . . . " where the verb already expresses the sense of the adjective.

Swollen sentences heave into view: "The administration is going ahead despite the fact that opposition in Congress is rising." That should have been ". . . despite rising congressional opposition," if the writer had stayed awake.

Even stranger: "Good military and business strategy dictate avoidance of any action that places one in a position where others can call the shots." In his better moments, the writer would say, ". . . dictate that you keep the upper hand." Nine words saved.

And nearly inscrutable: "Yet, he said, humans oddly realize their limited finitude, and by the very fact that they do, transcend it in awareness of some further being of potential infinity." These are the problems which, in our limited finitude, we create for ourselves. (Another is journalese, our own tribal dialect, which is the subject of a later chapter.) But journalists also are professionally exposed to language bloat, jargons pumped into the atmosphere by official news sources and "communicators" in the bureaucracy, the professions, institutions, corporations.

Reporters are obligated to translate gobbledygook into plain English. Yet often they get stuck in the viscous verbiage of their sources. Even in the reporting on schools, a subject close to so many readers, pedagogue's jargon oozes into print. Libraries are promoted to *resource centers.* Classrooms become *classroom situations,* and classes become *learning experiences.* Kids who won't study are *underachievers.* The teacher's effort to encourage them becomes *an attempt to raise motivational levels.* The principal who wants calm in the classroom *proposes viable new goals in behavior modification.* Little Marsha's shyness is *difficulty to relate to her peer group.* None of this does much for the writer, and does much less for Mrs. Jones, the reader who wants to know what's going on in her local school.

The fatal lure of wordiness, abstraction and jargon is hardly new. More than 40 years ago George Orwell, a master of the plain, forceful style, deplored the same tendencies.

Contemporary writing at its worst, he noted in his essay on "Politics and the English Language," doesn't choose words for the sake of their meaning but consists of "gumming long strips of words together that have already been set in order by someone else." He translated a verse from Ecclesiastes to illustrate the prose this leads to:

> I returned and saw under the sun, that the race is not to the swift, nor the battle to the strong, neither yet bread to the wise, nor yet riches to men of understanding, nor yet favor to men of skill; but time and chance happeneth to them all.

In modern bureaucratese:

> Objective consideration of contemporary phenomena compel the conclusion that success or failure in competitive activities exhibits no tendency to be commensurate with innate capacity, but that a considerable element of the unpredictable must invariably be taken into account.

This is parody, but not greatly overdrawn. A CEO speaks of "restructuring corporate culture" and "anticipated synergistic impacts on future profitability and employment levels." He's a cackle away from a federal agency's brand of horses and hens: "Grain-consuming animal units." A parachute drop on Grenada was a "predawn vertical insertion." A civilian type came up with "fourth-quarter equity retreat" for the '87 stock market crash. And what's death on the operating table but a "substantive negative outcome?"

No one has appointed journalists as the guardians of the language, which goes its own way anyhow. But self-preservation should prompt us to combat imbecilities in our own copy. Our treasury is words. We can't afford to convert them into non-performing assets, in the bankers' delicate phrase.

And we are free to choose, to avoid hand-me-down phrases, official cant, the staccato of journalese. Our words then will be measured to how things really happen, how they really look and feel.

Take the following example. AP staffer Leslie Dreyfous introduces an "issue story" with simple particulars and in plain language:

BROCKTON, Mass. (AP)—Sometimes, Mary Freeland looks at her son and remembers the kid who used to coast his bike down Colonel Bell Drive to the whoops of the neighborhood gang.

But then she looks again and reality crashes in: It's two decades later, and he still is that child.

It's two decades later, and Mary is back to being a full-time mother, six years after she placed her son in a school for the mentally retarded and began a new life. The state has run out of money and Patrick, along with hundreds of other adults like him, has been sent home.

"I'm a grandmother," said Mary, whose eldest daughter, Molly, has a son. "And I'm raising a child I'll be raising forever, starting all over again."

Similar troubles affect more than 63,000 families nationwide, the U.S. Association for Retarded Citizens says. . . .

And here, under deadline pressure amid bloodshed and chaos, AP Special Correspondent Mort Rosenblum reports on the Romanian uprising:

BUCHAREST, Romania (AP)—The Romanian faithful today are celebrating the Christmas miracle that freed them from a Communist dictator who trampled religious freedom and even kept Christmas music off the radio.

"There were so many years when I did not come to church for fear of the government," said one worshiper, Victoria Ionita, on Christmas Eve. "Now there is shooting in the streets, but I come because of trust in God."

Christmas music rang out Sunday throughout Romania for the first time since Communists took over in 1947.

Fighting raged on between soldiers backing the provisional government and security forces loyal to dictator Nicolae Ceausescu, who was ousted Friday and later arrested.

A few families carried freshly cut Christmas trees through Bucharest early Sunday. Sniper fire quickly cleared the streets.

For many Romanians, Ceausescu's downfall was a Christmas miracle from St. Dimitrius, the 12th-century holy man whose relics lay in the gilded and frescoed cathedral the deposed dictator wanted to destroy. . . .

BUCHAREST, Romania (AP)—At graveside, a yellow bath towel knotted around a rough pine cross and a spray of white chrysanthemums scrounged in a city where even bread is scarce were among tributes to heroes of the revolution.

A procession of sobbing families Tuesday accompanied makeshift coffins to a field of 200 freshly dug gaves in southern Bucharest. One coffin was for 14-year-old Silviu Minca. His friends said he was killed when the nation's hated security police called to them from a window and opened fire.

The security police have killed hundreds, perhaps thousands in their armed resistance to the uprising.

By a pine cross marked "first hero," a veteran gravedigger named Nicolae Abag wept along with the mourners.

"This is so, so much," he said. "I have not cried here since the earth moved in 1977," the year of the earthquake in which almost 2,000 people were killed.

All this is straightforward and effective. No clichés, no superlatives; just the sort of detail that will make readers see as well as understand.

Not every news subject can be handled in exactly that style, but all news writing should aim for similar simplicity and directness. That is the message of this book. The rest is amplification.

NEWS WRITING: Information Is Not Enough

Someone once asked Ernest Hemingway why he had kept doggedly rewriting the final chapter of *A Farewell to Arms*—supposedly 44 times. The answer: "To get the words right."

It's always a bit of a struggle to get the words right, whether we're a Hemingway or a few fathoms below his level. What first springs to mind is seldom good enough. Writing is the art of the second thought.

The humble grunts of daily journalism work under constraints that novelists don't have to worry about, but some second thought there must be—even if only for a few minutes when time is short, as it often is.

To gather information is not enough; we must also get people to read it. Only six adults in 10 read daily newspapers in these days of the video generation. "Reader-friendly" has become a catchword in publishing circles.

We can do without the phrase, but what's meant is clear: You must write *to* readers, not at them, in language attuned to their lives and everyday experience—language plain but not dull, terse yet relaxed, standard English that's correct but neither stilted nor high-flown. There may be easier ways to make a living, but then what's more satisfying than the craft, the art, of storytelling, which is what we do when at our best?

Clarity, precision, a sense for detail and other virtues needed to see us through rarely arrive unbidden. They must be coaxed and nurtured.

For a start, news writers should ask themselves three questions before letting go of a story:

1. Have I said what I meant to say? The writer of the following sentence didn't quite make it:

Covenant House later conceded that it had provided the young man, Kevin White, with a new identity, using the birth certificate of a 10-year-old boy who died in 1980 without permission from the child's parents.

2. Have I put it as concisely as possible? The writer of the following sentence, from a story about a California brushfire, may well have thought so:

Twelve rescue ambulances stood by to rush injured persons to nearby hospitals.

But on second thought it becomes clear that eight of those 12 words are drones. Ambulances are rescue vehicles; they don't dawdle; they always carry the injured, not the hale and hearty; and they rarely search for the remoter hospitals. Four words are all you needed: *Twelve ambulances stood by.*

3. Have I put things as simply as possible?

The relationship between Congress and bureaucrats is one of symbiosis.

Sure, the word fits nicely, and it's fine for some audiences. But how many ordinary readers would understand it? So why not say, "feed off each other" or "depend on each other"? The phrases give the sense in plain language.

The company expects significant synergy from the merger.

Synergy is a corporate buzzword (and seldom an actual result). Longer but less mysterious:

The company expects that the joined businesses will be more productive than the sum of their parts.

Details, you might say. But attention to detail is at the heart of good writing. As a sports announcer might say, it's a game of inches. Get careless with clauses and a sentence turns into a black hole from which no light escapes. Misplace a modifier and a serious passage becomes a grinning farce. Let an indefinite pronoun float free of its moorings, and you create a mystery about who does what to whom.

There's no solace in the thought that many readers will be able to figure out a muddled sentence. They should not be asked to. They should not be required to guess, to pause, to backtrack, or slog through a swamp of superfluous words. They'll find better things to do.

Wasted Words, Wasted Space

Nowhere is the case for economy with words stated more persuasively than in *The Elements of Style* by William Strunk and E.B. White:

> Vigorous writing is concise. A sentence should contain no unnecessary words, a paragraph no unnecessary sentences, for the same reason that a drawing should contain no unnecessary lines and a machine no unnecessary parts. This requires not that a writer make all his sentences short, or that he avoid all detail and treat his subject only in outline, but that every word tell.

All news writers past their novitiate understand the need to save words, but many of us are voluble by nature.

It's a matter of habit, starting with the small, innocuous phrase: *in the event of* for *if, despite the fact that* for *in spite of, adverse weather conditions* for *bad weather, take into custody* for *arrest.*

Many sentences can be improved by surface trimming. In the following example, just omit the italicized words:

> WASHINGTON—The Reagan administration is writing *new* regulations *designed* to sweep away many years of *accumulated* red tape and let local governments decide *for themselves* how to spend major urban aid grants.

Often, slight rewording produces dramatic results. Compare the original sentence (left) with the revision on the right:

It is unusual in the Legislature to have a conference with more than four members.	A conference committee with more than four members is unusual.
The IRS said that a number of Oregon complaints had been received as of Friday. Investigators are now in the process of checking out the possible violations.	The IRS said a number of Oregon complaints had been received as of Friday. Investigators are checking them.
Consumers were slower in repaying installment debt in August and quicker in adding new debt in August than earlier this year, the government reported.	Consumers were quicker to borrow and slower to repay in August than earlier this year, the government reported.

Six, seven and six words are saved, respectively. The shorter versions are crisper. Eliminating tedium and saving words go hand in hand:

Israel *is not in favor of* a Mideast peace conference.	. . . opposes . . .
The Senate Ethics Committee can vote *for the expulsion of* . . .	. . . to expel . . .
The union will *conduct a poll of* its members.	. . . poll . . .
The Iranians hope *for the re-equipment of* their armed forces.	. . . to re-equip . . .

Every day's news copy throws up a flock of short phrases which, on second thought, prove inflated. Here's a sampling of what writers said and what, in the context, they meant:

announced the names of	identified
Detroit area residential and real estate holding	houses in the Detroit area
responds specifically to incidents	responds to incidents

for the entire distance of the flight	for the flight
use his persuasive powers on behalf of	support
not yet known	unknown
can produce liver degeneration	can damage the liver
so it can afford to re-equip its fleet with new fuel-efficent jets	so it can buy fuel-efficient jets
now is asking for the relaxation of	wants to relax

The Anemia of Abstractions

Certain abstract nouns, perennials of newspaper usage, tend to create clusters of surplus words: *issue, case, situation, question, condition, facilities, activities, experience, field, factor, proposition, basis, character, nature, process, problem.* Often these nouns are tacked onto specific words: heavy traffic becomes *a heavy traffic problem* or *the congested traffic situation.*

Besides being stuffy, these nouns are vague. What is a facility, an issue, a problem? A facility can be an airport, a hotel, a park or a kitchen. An issue is anything people discuss or disagree about. A health problem can be an ingrown toenail or terminal cancer.

A man who gets his throat slit in a dark alley is *a victim of violence*, but much is lost in the transcription. That is how abstract words work. Call a spade a spade and you evoke a clear picture. Call it an agricultural implement and you might be talking about a plow, a rake, or an air-conditioned tractor.

Obviously these long-faced, abstract nouns have some use, but the following examples show why you should treat them with reserve:

The *situation* poses a danger to the public because of the tendency of persons on probation to commit more crimes.	It's risky because people on probation often commit crimes.
On the *issue* of welfare payments, the committee deferred action for three weeks.	The committee deferred action on welfare payments for three weeks.

The government decided to replace him with a general of more aggressive *character*.

. . . replace him with a more aggressive general.

Crimes of a violent *nature* are increasing.

Violent crimes are increasing.

The Legislature has threatened to suspend all strip mining *operations*.

. . . all strip mining.

Ample space for recreational *activities* was provided.

Ample space for recreation was provided.

The bridge below Smithville has now become a practical *proposition*.

. . . has become feasible.

The loss of skilled workers will be a crippling *factor* in the economy of East Germany.

. . . will cripple the economy of East Germany.

Another worrisome matter is the *question* of productivity.

Another worry is productivity.

They receive their checks on a monthly *basis*.

They receive monthly checks.

They agreed that their adventure in the woods had been a worthwhile *experience*.

. . . had been worthwhile.

Mathematics skills are considered a valuable learning *experience*.

They can learn much from mathematics.

He is an acknowledged leader in the medical *field*.

He is a leader in medicine.

Half of the town lives in *conditions* of abject poverty.

. . . lives in abject poverty.

The state's hospital *facilities* must be upgraded.

The state's hospitals must be upgraded.

The prepositional phrase *in terms of* enjoys a peculiar vogue today, perhaps because of its technical aura. Useful in expressing some relationships—*The dollar is worth less in terms of the Japanese yen*—it is frequently used in ways that turn sentences into fudge:

He would not predict the effect of service cuts *in terms of* revenues and riderships.	He would not predict how service cuts would affect revenues and ridership.
The company pledged improvements *in terms of* labor relations and efficiency.	The company pledged to improve labor relations and efficiency.

People Power

Under the heading of "abstractitis," Fowler's *Dictionary of Modern English Usage* says: "Persons and what they do, things and what is done to them are put in the background and we can only peer at them as through a glass darkly."

Here are some examples:

Research has shown that accidents are proportionately more prevalent with motorcycle use and are of a more violent nature.

Nothing in that sentence acts on anything. There's no hint that it has anything to do with people. Put more concretely:

Motorcyclists *have more accidents proportionately than other* motorists and are more often killed or seriously injured, research has shown.

A state civil service examination to fill uniformed court officers' jobs "had grossly disproportionate impact on blacks and Hispanics as compared to whites," it was charged in a federal court suit today.	A state civil service examination to fill jobs for uniformed court officers was unfair to blacks and Hispanics, a federal court suit charged today.

The revision at right takes two words, *was unfair*, to say what the original version says in 13. Note also how the unpleasant noun pileup, *uniformed court officers jobs*, is loosened up with a preposition.

Utilities were under mandate Wednesday not to cut off services during the winter months to *elderly individuals whose health might thus be endangered.*	Utilities were under orders Wednesday not to cut off services to the elderly and seriously ill.

The revision specifies who is meant.

Here are abstract blotches in an action story:

Police are "furious" over *a recent rash of objects* being thrown from highway overpasses at moving vehicles and say they are going to crack down on the *offenders* "before someone gets killed."

Police Detective John Smith said police have not been able to link recent wrecks involving serious injuries to the *overpass offenses* but added: "We just think that some recent accidents are related to this. It just seems too much of a coincidence."

As the story notes later, the little monsters were tossing bottles, rocks and bricks, which is livelier than *recent rash of objects*. Let details drive out generalities:

Police say they are furious at youngsters tossing rocks and bottles from overpasses and intend to crack down "before some driver gets killed."

Detective John Smith said police have been unable to link recent serious accidents to the rock throwers, "but it just seems like too much of a coincidence."

It's possible to be too specific, though, especially in crime and accident stories. Gory details don't necessarily add much except revulsion.

When a body long dead is recovered, it's superfluous to mention that it was *badly decomposed*. Nor was it useful to report, in a plane crash story, that *the flesh fell off some of the victims* who burned to death. *Charred beyond recognition* is another phrase you can usually dispense with. A man stabbed 20 times may be presumed to have bled; the writer need not dwell on the dimensions of a *pool of blood*. Limit the gore. For that matter, you often find a crime victim described as *fully clothed*, gratuitous when there is no reason to suspect otherwise.

You can't avoid abstractions entirely. Some stories must be carried on in abstract terms; try to lighten them with concrete illustrations. And abstract words save time and space on second and further references. That's fine, so long as they are preceded by particulars.

The following story, though, is the kind of disaster that happens when all defenses fail:

LARAMIE, Wyo.—A University of Wyoming trustee committee has given its approval to drafts of reallocation criteria and processes de-.spite concern over just who will be allowed to influence the process.

The Academic Issues Committee approved the drafts during the first day of the trustees' two-day meeting.

Some trustees want input from outside the university personnel rolls, but at least one member of the administration said he is concerned over the possible impact that might have.

Trustee President Ford Bussart said he wants students and community members to have a say in the reallocation process because he thinks they will have valuable input.

"There are items and matters which may not appear to have importance, which in fact, if viewed from other perspectives on the part of interested constituencies, indeed have importance," the Green River attorney said. "I simply fear that if we internalize the process completely and don't get those external points of view, we can find this process becomes nearly impossible to accomplish. Which can create problems for the university."

What's being reallocated? Who might influence the "process" and how? What are the "criteria?" Does "personnel rolls" mean the faculty or anybody employed by the school? What are the "items and matters" referred to in the fifth graf? There's no way for the reader to dispel the fog.

Academics are among the worst perpetrators of gobbledygook known on this planet. That's their problem. When we fail to translate, it becomes ours.

Hold the Adjectives

Not every noun needs an adjective. Not every adjective needs an adverb. Not every writer has got the message.

E. B. White once observed that the adjective hasn't been born yet that can pull a noun out of a tight spot. Mark Twain, who also had writing experience, once told a young correspondent, "When you can catch an adjective, kill it."

He softened that a little: "No, I don't mean that utterly, but kill the most of them—then the rest will be valuable. They weaken when they are close together, they give strength when wide apart.

An adjective habit, or a wordy, flowery, diffuse habit, once fastened upon a person is as hard to get rid of as any other vice."

Some writers think killing adjectives is like clubbing baby seals; they can't bear the thought. But strong writing should rely on nouns and verbs. Pick the right ones and you'll need few modifiers. Use adjectives to make your meaning clear, not as decorative afterthoughts.

It is hard to see what the second adjective is doing in this sentence:

> The shots on the quiet Sunday morning sent passersby into *frightened* flight.

Quiet, yes. But *frightened* flight? As distinguished from courageous flight?

The lust for modification leads writers into other futilities. Certain nouns evoke inevitable adjectives that are only feebly descriptive. The combinations become clichés: *Posh* resort, *sprawling* reservation, *hardy* natives, *devout* Catholic, *scenic* countryside, *colorful* scene, *high-powered* rifle, *picturesque* village, and many more.

An onslaught of modifiers turns the following story into treacle:

> LONDON—The *slim, almost boyish* figure of the next king of England moved across the *thick* carpet of the *elegant* Brown's Hotel at Piccadilly. He signed the hotel register as cameras flashed.
>
> En route back to the *enormous, black* Rolls Royce outside, he suddenly stopped. He had spotted two young women working on a guest register in the lobby.
>
> "What are you doing?" he inquired *politely* in *deep aristocratic* tones.
>
> The receptionists looked up and their jaws fell.
>
> "The guest register, is it?" asked the *immaculately groomed* Prince Charles.

You would expect a prince to be polite and immaculately groomed and to visit an elegant hotel rather than a fleabag. Anyway, *thick carpet* suggests elegance. And what is *almost boyish*? What are *deep aristocratic tones*? Strike all modifiers except *thick, enormous, black,* and *slim,* and the intro recovers.

Keep your hands off nouns that need no additional voltage: *serious* danger, *stern* warning, *deadly* poison, *grave* crisis. The nouns do better without the modifiers.

A crisis is a serious turning point by definition. And the habit of mechanical modifying leads to many glaring redundancies, among them:

absolutely conclusive	lifeless corpse
agricultural crops	meaningless gibberish
awkward dilemma	mutual cooperation
close proximity	new record
complete monopoly	old adage
completely full	organic life
divisive quarrel	original founder
end result	patently obvious
entirely absent	personal friend
exact counterpart	personal opinion
future plan	pragmatic realist
general public	present incumbent
grateful thanks	sworn affidavit
hired mercenary	true facts
irreducible minimum	ultimate outcome
lonely hermit	violent explosion

To test the logic of such modifiers, turn them around. Are there gentle explosions? Pleasant dilemmas? False facts? Impersonal friends?

Treat adverbial intensifiers with the same caution as adjectives. *Very urgent, highly unusual, extremely serious*—the adverbs add only shrillness. *Definitely* is generally expendable. *The ambassador will definitely leave tomorrow* says nothing more than that he'll leave. *Undue* can be particularly fatuous:

State officials expressed the hope that people in the New Madrid area would show no *undue* alarm over the earthquake prediction.

What's due alarm? ". . . would remain calm."

The conservative group complained that the court was taking *undue* liberties with the Constitution.

Strike *undue*. Adverbs like *relatively* and *comparatively* are usually mere padding:

Relatively few senators answered the quorum call.

The number of football injuries is *comparatively* high this year.

Relative to or compared with what?

Qualifiers: Hedge If You Must

Qualifiers are necessary in statements open to doubt. Because news reports are often based on partial information, some hedging is inevitable: *Possibly, perhaps, probably, allegedly, reportedly, on the whole*, and so on.

Some writers are so addicted—or so insecure—that they guard their flanks with qualifiers even when the flank needs no guarding.

Dingell, it can *probably* be said with *absolute certainty* . . .

Either *probably* or *absolute certainty* but not both.

Both men pleaded guilty to the *alleged* theft of $40,000.

Since they pleaded guilty, "alleged" is unneeded.

Patrons at the restaurant told police the *suspect* had methodically relieved them of their wallets and valuables. He then *allegedly* took the contents of the cash register and escaped through a side door.

Since the robber is not named, both "allegedly" and "suspect" are unnecessary, unless the writer suspected the victims of hallucinating.

Here's a case of a modifier, itself unnecessary, qualified into never-never land:

Saudi Arabia's *almost* single-minded obsession with security . . .

An obsession implies single-mindedness. You're either single-minded or you aren't. If the writer suspected his assertion, he should have made the noun *preoccupation* and scuttled the adjective and adverb.

Look hard at *basically, essentially, fundamentally* & Co., which are usually superfluous.

Basically, Sears is changing its price policy.

In a news story, you're not expected to give every aspect of the company's plan. If what you left out is important, put it in. If not, forget the qualifier.

They are called something else here, but *essentially* they work as security guards.

If that's what they do essentially, good enough:

While they are called something else, they work as security guards.

In *simplest terms*, the heart acts like a pump.

That may imply to touchy readers that they couldn't follow you if you let yourself go. Anyway, you're supposed to write in simplest (but not oversimplified) terms.
Potential and *possible* often seem pointless.

City negotiators are trying to head off a possible strike by teachers next week . . .

They want to prevent a real strike, not a possible one.

The intention is to discourage *potential* attacks against oil installations . . .

They want to discourage the genuine article.
Arguably, now popular, is usually meaningless. Almost anything is arguable.

Leonard Bernstein was *arguably* one of the most dazzling musicians America has produced.

Make it *perhaps* or *probably*.

Put Verbs to Work

The verb, particularly in the active voice, is ringmaster of the sentence. It sets pace and movement. A peculiarity of abstract writing is an aversion to strong verbs, which are thinned out into combinations of weak verb, abstract noun and modifier.

In the following sentences, the revision on the right shows the magic of verbs properly used:

The refugees *experienced severe hunger* in their wilderness retreat.	The refugees starved in their wilderness retreat.

Portland *showed a collective grief* over the deaths of the young climbers.	Portland grieved over the deaths of the young climbers.

Other symptoms of noun disease:

determined the truth of	verified
gave permission to	permitted
held a meeting	met
proved of benefit to	benefited
put in an appearance	appeared
reached an agreement	agreed
submitted his resignation	resigned
take into consideration	consider
established conclusive evidence of	proved
take into custody	arrest, seize

Occasionally the wordier form is justified to capture a nuance. *Reach an agreement* suggests a longer effort, perhaps, than *agree*. Usually, however, the single verb will do.

Effect and *impact* devour more precise verbs:

Teachers as well as parents have much *impact* on students' career choices.	. . . influence students' career choices.
The boycott had no *effect* on sales.	. . . did not reduce sales.
The prosecutor's statement had an obvious *effect* on the jury.	. . . swayed the jury.

Be Short, Familiar, Specific

From what we have seen about clutter, vagueness and officialese, certain precepts arise. They were derived long ago from the practice of good writers. Consider them a charm against the legion of devils that forever try to turn prose into slush:

Prefer the short word to the long.
Prefer the familiar word to the fancy.
Prefer the specific word to the abstract.
Use no more words than necessary to make your meaning clear.

This does not mean that long or unfamiliar words should never be used. Sometimes they fit the meaning best. Occasionally they serve the rhythm of a sentence. But there must be good reasons for the choice. It's hard to see much advantage to long words such as those in the left-hand column:

accommodations	rooms
ameliorate	improve
approximately	about
assistance	help
commence	begin
deactivate	close, shut off
endeavor	try
finalize	end, complete
implement	carry out
in consequence of	because
initiate	begin
methodology	method
motivation	motive
objective	aim, goal
peruse	read
prior to	before
proliferation	spread
purchase	buy
remuneration	pay
replicate	repeat
socialize	mingle, meet, make friends
substantial proportion	many, much
underprivileged	poor
utilize	use

Corral Those Modifiers

The language has many ways to trip you up, most deviously through a modifier that turns up in the wrong place. Don't let related ideas in a sentence drift apart. Modifiers should be close to the word they modify, and verbs should be close to the subject.

Gorbachev was last seen in public Aug. 7, when he received a group of U.S. teachers of the Russian language in Moscow.

They may have been hard up over there, but Russian they knew. (. . . seen in public in Moscow Aug. 7 . . .)

Police hope an autopsy will confirm the identity of a teen-age boy whose body they found stuffed into a septic tank with the help of a self-proclaimed clairvoyant.

Back to the drawing board. (". . . whose body they found in a septic tank . . . ") Stuff it later.

A 6-year-old dog named Rosie has been honored by the American Humane Association for saving the life of her iron lung bound owner during a power outage with gifts of plaques and flowers and all the dog biscuits she could eat.

That must have done the patient a wealth of good.

A Harlem man who disappeared a month ago was found slain by his wife in the trunk of the couple's car, police said.

She's innocent. "A Harlem woman found the body of her slain husband in the trunk of their car, police said. He disappeared a month ago."
And those infamous dangling participles still claim victims:

While eating dinner in a hotel restaurant later, a boyish-looking, pink-skinned man with premature gray hair and dressed in a blue jump suit bounded up to the table.

Interesting, but poor for the digestion.

Already wheezing and short of breath, the principles of sound mountaineering were forgotten as they began their retreat.

As well they might be.

Who's Who?

Pronoun pain ensues from placement that leaves the antecedent in doubt:

He said he is certain it's an original de Torres painting, worth $200,000. The artist's signature is on it and *it* includes the faces of his favorite models, he said.

The pronoun *it* refers to *painting*, not the signature, which would have been worth $200,000 by itself with all those faces in it. Also, at first glance *he said* seems to refer to the dead artist, not the curator who was speaking.

The foreman told reporters later the jurors had trouble believing the state's witnesses. "They were confused on most major points," he said.

"They" can be read as referring to the jury. Putting "witnesses" in brackets after "they" is not the best solution. Make it: Their testimony "was confused on most major points," he said.

The Elegant Variation

Writers who believe that the repetition of plain words within shouting distance of each other is crude take off on synonym safaris. The practice was long ago ridiculed by Fowler, who named it "elegant variation." It's all the more grotesque as there are few true synonyms and the author introduces misfits:

> The mayor's task force was asked to meet with the owners of the *structures*, discuss whether they wanted their *buildings* preserved, and recommend ways to adapt older *edifices* to new use.

Structures could be anything and *edifices* is too grandiose; the story concerns commercial and apartment buildings.

If the writer didn't want to repeat *buildings*, a pronoun was the way out:

> . . . to meet with the owners of the buildings, discuss whether they wanted *them* preserved, and recommend ways to adapt the older ones to new uses.

The same craving for daintiness will convert elephants to *pachyderms*, dogs to *canines*, cats to *felines*, tigers to *striped predators*, cars to *vehicles*. Petroleum becomes *black gold*, snow becomes *white powder* (a justly forgotten poet once called it "*God's dandruff*"), a banana turns into *the elongated yellow fruit*.

The most common and perhaps most obnoxious form of the elegant variation consists in substitutions for a news subject's name. John Doe, president of Chapter 11 Bank, is reintroduced in successive paragraphs as *the ruddy-faced financier, the Hawaii native, the silver-haired executive*, and *the no-nonsense banker*.

If you know followers of this cult, deprogram them.

Avoid Palling Passives

Use the active voice whenever possible. *Police arrested John Smith* is shorter and crisper than *John Smith was arrested by police*. On many occasions, of course, news values dictate the passive form, in leads especially. If you were writing about your town's leading citizen, you'd make it *Mayor* John Smith was arrested by Smithtown police today.

In most cases, though, the passive is flabby, dropping the doer of a deed out of the picture.* That's why officialese favors the passive mode. *It is believed* or *it is estimated* allows the estimator and the believer to vanish in the fog.

Other things being equal, the passive almost always loses out to the active form:

Lighted candles were carried by most of the demonstrators in Prague, and elsewhere there were silent demonstrations by large crowds.	Most of the demonstrators carried lighted candles in Prague that night, and elsewhere large crowds also demonstrated silently.

Always distrust "there were," "there is," especially at the start of a sentence. There is usually—oops! You can usually find a better way. Forms of the verb *to be* offer little action. Saying that something exists is wetwash.

There was no one in the group of bystanders who came to the victim's aid.	No one in the group of bystanders helped him.

A sentence should be emphatic. When possible, express even a negative in positive form:

The Legislature did not consider the governor's proposal.	The Legislature ignored the governor's proposal.
The company said not all absentees had no excuse.	The company said some absentees had excuses.

---

*Some years ago, a specialist in the analysis of extortion notes and terrorist threats told an interviewer that a note that says "I will kill you" suggests the writer means business. "You will be killed," on the other hand, suggests that the writer may waver, lacking "sufficient commitment to identify himself as the agency of the threat."

Mismanaged Background

Badly placed background detail in a story often produces sentences with wildly disparate ideas. *Born in Detroit, he was an ardent stamp collector* is the kind of non sequitur one finds in many obituaries. The havoc caused by background material worked in without regard for logic and relevance is shown in the following passages from a second-day story on Elvis Presley's death.

The story goes back years, but it's such a classic of disheveled backgrounding that it's worth exhuming. Besides, you can show it to people who insist that Elvis is still alive, something the autopsy story seems to disprove.

The writer struggles to tell essentials of the singer's career within the framework of developing news, and some of the sentences flop around like beached fish:

Dr. George Nichopulos, longtime physician to the swivel-hipped, throaty baritone who was known as the King of Rock 'n' Roll, said an autopsy revealed a constriction in one of the arteries to the heart, which restricted blood flow and brought on a heart attack.

Presley, whose recording of "Heartbreak Hotel" helped put him on top of the entertainment world 21 years ago, was discovered unconscious at Graceland in suburban Memphis Tuesday afternoon.

The doctor said attempts to revive Presley, who appeared in 31 films—including "Love Me Tender" and "Jailhouse Rock"—continued because of a slight chance that life still existed in his body.

In the next example, too, misplaced details interfere with the flow of thought. The story is about a man who survived a long fall when his parachute failed to open.

The son of a postal worker, Mongillo was living in Florida when he had his brush with death.

Mongillo, whose only income is $100 a month from a local welfare fund, said, "I was scared. I knew I was going to die."

The answer to such difficulties is to disengage and regroup. In the Presley story, the facts about his death, the resuscitation effort and the autopsy belong in one section of the story, the facts of his rise to fame, film credits and song hits in another. In the Mongillo story, a separate paragraph should have wrapped up his postal antecedents and poverty.

Where background details can be woven smoothly into the narrative, it's the preferred way. Where they chop up the story and the logic of individual sentences, it's best to present the material in a coherent paragraph or two at an appropriate place in the story.

Useful as the inverted pyramid is—and indispensable for fast-breaking stories—it presents a risk. The sequence of central events is sometimes left foggy. Readers are told what happened, but not always how, in what order. Careful writers will sort it out in a clear, chronological summary somewhere in the story after they have disposed of the main news points. Often matters are left like this:

> Wielding homemade knives, the inmates commandeered a milk truck, which they used to vault over a 25-foot wall, he said. The group then threw Molotov cocktails made with paint thinner at a guard tower and leaped from the top of the truck.

When did they vault? When did they leap?

In the following example, a simple sequence becomes twisted by needless *befores* and *afters*:

Last Wednesday, the 3-year-old monkey escaped from a backyard leash and bit a woman and her son *after* jumping into their passing car.	Last Wednesday, Columbo slipped his leash and escaped from Coleman's backyard.
Neighbor Debbie Jackson testified that, *before* the attack, the monkey was taunted by several youths who raced at it with bicycles and screamed.	A neighbor testified that screaming youngsters raced at Columbo with their bicycles. The frightened monkey jumped into a passing car and bit the driver and her son.
After the biting, Columbo climbed into a tree and descended only *after* a boy coaxed him down with sliced bananas.	Columbo then climbed into a tree and stayed there until a boy coaxed him down with banana slices.

Clean and lean sentences flourish best in a well-organized story. Mishandling of background gums up the machinery. That is largely a matter of organization. Jumping back and forth results in excess wordage and tires the reader. Complete each topic before going on to the next.

In structure and sentence: Simplify. Avoid clutter. Prune. Think twice.

LEADS: The Agony of Square One

3

In the beginning of every news story is the lead—the bait, the lure, the tender trap for the reader, a source of much fear and loathing for the writer.

Like a fiddle string, a good lead is the product of the right tension. Or, to get the metaphors out of the way, the lead is an hors d'oeuvre, supposed to whet the appetite, not to provide a three-course dinner.

Don't be intimidated by leads, however. Think of them as though they cost you 10 bucks per word, each word to be engraved on stainless steel while you're sitting on a hot stove. Think economy.

A good lead makes a clear statement of the essential news point and when possible includes a detail that distinguishes the story from others of its kind. If the bank robbers escaped *in a baby blue Mercedes*, that small fact belongs in the lead.

Leads should be clear and specific; they must not mumble. Mumblers stem from various defects:

- A gaggle of secondary detail
- Abstract and general language
- Vagueness
- Stress on how something is announced rather than what is said, or on how the news originates rather than the news itself
- Entanglement in the chronology of an event

Don't Bury the News

To avoid mumblers, the lead writer must first of all decide what the most important news is, which can be difficult in situations where much is happening. The following mammoth evades that rule and dooms itself:

WASHINGTON—Sen. Dave Durenberger, acknowledging that depositions in the ethics case against him appear to support key allegations, has canceled a 10-day trip to Moscow because of time spent on what he insists will be a strong defense to present to the Senate Ethics Committee.

Well, what's most important here? The cancelation of the trip? The acknowledgment? The bit about the strong defense? One or two knitted together, but not everything.

Two of several possibilities:

WASHINGTON—Sen. Dave Durenberger has canceled a 10-day trip to Moscow because of the time consumed by preparations for his defense in an ethics case.

Or:

Sen. Dave Durenberger has acknowledged that depositions in the ethics case against him appear to support key allegations but says he will have a strong defense.

The next lead takes a long scenic route and smothers the news beneath 47 words and a colon.

In a landmark legal case that took the emotional right-to-die issue from a snowy country road in rural Missouri to the halls of the Supreme Court in Washington, a county probate judge issued what is likely to be the final ruling in the matter yesterday: he authorized the family of Nancy Beth Cruzan to stop having chemical nutrition and water pumped into the comatose woman's stomach.

This gets to the point more quickly:

A county probate judge in Missouri authorized the family of Nancy Beth Cruzan yesterday to discontinue medical intervention and allow her to die after seven years in an irreversible coma.

Here's a lead that starts out strongly enough but fades near the end:

The City Council has passed a law banning families with children aged 14 or under from certain parts of town.

Certain parts? Care to say which? Near the old swimming hole perhaps? Well, residential communities for senior citizens. That's what the lead should have specified, along with other material found down in the story:

> Landlords in senior citizens' communities who sell or rent to families with young children face jail terms and fines under an ordinance passed by the City Council.

Here is a terminal mumbler. Only one word has a semblance of news interest, and it is hard to spot amid the debris:

> Rep. Ken Hechler, D-W.Va., said a decision Wednesday by the U.S. Court of Appeals that gives the go-ahead for the construction of the Blue Ridge power project on the New River is "ridiculous."

Just clearing away the clutter couldn't salvage that opener. You have to exhume an angle from the next-to-last graf of the story:

> Rep. Ken Hechler says people in West Virginia and two other states will mobilize to protect the New River after Wednesday's "ridiculous" court decision approving the Blue Ridge power project.

Too Much, Too Little

Following are some typical leads, long and short, that say too much. A trimmed version is on the right.

WASHINGTON—The Federal Trade Commission agreed Friday to allow the nation's biggest leveraged buyout to go through, provided the two corporations involved—which together account for one-eighth of the food sold in the nation's supermarkets — reduce their share of the markets for ketchup, Oriental foods and packaged nuts.

WASHINGTON—The Federal Trade Commission agreed Friday to let the nation's biggest leveraged buyout go through if both corporations reduce their market share in ketchup, Oriental foods and packaged nuts.

PALM BEACH, Fla.—Israel remains America's most reliable

PALM BEACH, Fla.—Israel remains the most reliable U.S.

ally in the world, but it must recognize that the killing of Palestinian civilians in the strife-torn West Bank and Gaza Strip is "clearly unacceptable," Vice President Dan Quayle told a Jewish group today.

ally but must recognize that the killing of Palestinian civilians is "clearly unacceptable," Vice President Dan Quayle told a Jewish group today.

DALLAS—Mary Kay Cosmetics says it has placed a moratorium on using animals to verify the safety of its products.

DALLAS—Mary Kay Cosmetics says it has halted using animals to test product safety.

WASHINGTON—A fighter plane that combines long-range supersonic cruise capability with greatly enhanced ability to dogfight at and above the speed of sound has long been an elusive dream of aircraft engineers.

WASHINGTON—A supersonic plane built for long-range cruising and dogfights has long been a dream of aircraft designers.

The original carries a lethal dose of Pentagon jargon. And a long-held dream can't be anything but elusive.

The pruning knife is the remedy for verbose mumblers. There's no known cure for leads that say too little:

> Gov. Mario Cuomo and his three opponents cast the crime issue—the biggest concern of voters, according to polls—in different ways.

Goodbye, reader.

> ODON, Ind.—Vice Adm. John Poindexter's hometown was quiet Saturday night after his conviction on charges of conspiracy, obstruction and lying to Congress.

Did we expect riots or parades?

> MINOCQUA, Wis.—What can you do when a tornado has flattened much of an eight-year dream, killing one person and leaving a twisted shambles where your resort and North woods campground had been?

Start rebuilding, we'd say.

Try Writing "Visually"

You can avoid mumblers by being specific and concrete, giving the reader a picture. A clever phrase, a touch of humor, an ironic contrast help.

> MADISON, Wis. (AP)—State Sen. Clifford "Tiny" Krueger eased his 300-pound frame into a witness chair Friday and said fat people should not be barred from adopting children.

That little gem draws the reader right into the story. The next tells virtually a whole story in two short sentences:

> MIAMI (AP)—Bill Cashman, a fireman, says he didn't mind posing nude for a centerfold in a magazine for women who like men. But he has a $2 million objection to use of the picture by a magazine for men who like men.

It would be hard to stop reading here—as it would be after the following:

> MARIETTA, Ohio (AP)—His work done, his children grown, his age past 80, his days of toil to get ahead well behind, George Oakes nonetheless sat down one day and built a better mousetrap.

Next, two short leads (proving it doesn't take a lot of words to be effective).

> BOSTON (AP)—Here's an insight that may fail to shock dedicated students of the mating game: People often tell lies in order to have sex. Honest.

This dealt with one of those sociological studies that tell you what you've known all your life.

> BEIJING—China's decade-long shopping spree is over for now, squelched by a government austerity program that has pushed the nation precariously close to recession.

Homely language for complex economic developments. Even the shortest, simplest sort of lead can provide an alluring gateway, as the following from *USA Today* shows. It's about voters across the country turning down expensive programs:

> If it cost money, Tuesday's voters weren't buying.

What's the Difference?

The real key to lifting your lead out of the humdrum is to ask yourself what is *different* about each story.

Much of the news is repetitive: war, crime, disaster. The goal, both in the lead and in the rest of the story, is to stress those angles that are least like the routine of other stories in this class. Often this special element is there and writers overlook it and lose the chance to provide their lead with that small hook that grabs the reader.

> A car sliced through a crowded fast food restaurant at lunchtime Tuesday, officials said, killing two people and injuring six others.

Nothing wrong with that lead. Well, perhaps the attribution, *officials said*, could wait until the second paragraph since nothing in the story is in contention. In any case, a car smashing into a restaurant at lunchtime is news enough for a lead, you might say, and it is written clearly and succinctly.

But eight grafs into the story appears a tidbit of information from the coroner. The two killed were a husband and wife, ages 72 and 68, who had stopped "to have a sandwich before going to the funeral home down the street for the funeral of their son-in-law's uncle." Aha, the writer should have said, and written:

> YOUNGSTOWN, Ohio—A car sliced through a fast food restaurant Tuesday, killing an elderly couple who had stopped for lunch on the way to a family member's funeral. Six other people were injured.

Alert writers and editors will constantly watch for such distinctive particulars. More examples:

A report from New Zealand about a crazed shooter who killed 12 people in a remote hamlet. That's dramatic enough, but down in the fourth graf the story gave the population as 28 souls. The fact that the killer wiped out nearly half the population should have been in the lead.

> SAN FRANCISCO—Children as young as 3 years old were found working in violation of child-labor laws, the U.S. Department of Labor said.

Unaccountably deferred was a striking particular: They were found working in an onion field.

This lead came to AP's New York General Desk:

DENVER—About 150 soot-covered firefighters made headway Monday in curbing the spread of a fire burning 1.6 million gallons of jet fuel at a tank near Stapleton International Airport.

The editor found a small, glittering fact in the copy and revised:

DENVER—Patience, and a quarter of the water that Denver uses in one day, enabled firefighters to rein in a fire . . .

Sometimes a clever idea makes all the difference:

FRANKFORT, Ky. (AP)—Local school boards in Kentucky are being caught in the middle of a controversy over posting copies of the Ten Commandments in public school classrooms.

When the story arrived at the AP's General Desk in New York the lead was reshaped this way, taking advantage of a blessed opportunity:

FRANKFORT, Ky. (AP)—Thou shalt post the Ten Commandments on the classroom wall, says a 1978 Kentucky law. Thou shalt not, says the U.S. Supreme Court. Help! say confused local school boards.

Needless to say, cleverness demands caution. It is easy to slip over the line into the sophomoric.

HARTFORD, Conn.—Hello, tree. There is good news and there is bad news for you today.

That's plain silly.

Action Speaks Louder

The more action your lead conveys, the better. Strong verbs are important.

Verbs like *moved, scheduled, expected, prepared*, which so often crop up in second-day leads, are crutches. See what the good choice of verbs does for these leads:

NEW YORK—To the last day, Americans *flocked* to the tall ships at berth, *clambered up* the treacherous gangplanks, *grasped* the huge wheels, and *fondled* the brass windlasses.

FRANKLINTON, La.—A tank truck carrying 7,000 gallons of gasoline *collided* with a car and *overturned* Monday, crushing the trucker to death and igniting a fire that *spread* 50-foot flames over two blocks.

Following are three leads on the same subject. The first is pretty flat, relying on "linked" and ending lamely with "will result. . . ."

LONDON—Drillers working deep beneath the English Channel last night *linked* mainland Europe to Britain with a 2-inch-wide borehole *that will result* in a channel tunnel.

The second, by referring to the Ice Age, adds some color:

LONDON—Eight thousand years after the Ice Age put them asunder, Britain and France were *reunited* Tuesday beneath the English Channel.

But "reunited" is abstract and feeble. And were they really?
Despite its length—and maybe in this case because of it—the third lead is a success: "Mud-caked" and the list of previous failures give a nice twist to the phrase after the dash.

LONDON—A handful of mud-caked drillers working deep beneath the English Channel tonight succeeded where the Spanish Armada, Napoleon, Hitler and a small army of European Community bureaucrats all have tried and failed—they linked Britain to mainland Europe.

Pitfalls of Attribution

A common pitfall for the lead writer comes with attribution. Cattle may chew cud contentedly, but readers shouldn't be asked to digest the same bit of information several times within a few paragraphs. Such repetition is often due to clumsy structure, particularly in backing up or elaborating on the lead. Some writers have trouble introducing a new fact without swaddling it in information or phrases that have gone before. Double-decker leads result, the second or third graf saying much the same as the first.

The most common missteps are quotes which largely repeat what the lead has already told us:

LUBBOCK, Texas—School district officials were surprised by a judge's restraining order on the district's dress code, which allows boys with long hair and earrings to return to classes.

"We were somewhat surprised," said Mike Moses, superintendent of the Lubbock Independent School District.

WASHINGTON—The U.S. government is requiring some French and Italian vineyards to certify that wines imported by this country do not contain traces of a fungicide not approved in the United States.

"We have found a little bit of Italian wine and some French wine that contain traces of a fungicide not approved in the United States," Food and Drug Administration spokesman Bill Grigg said Sunday.

Another vintage double-decker:

Half of the Philadelphia Art Museum's permanent galleries were closed Sunday because of a shortage of security guards.

Museum officials said they had to close part of the museum because the city had not provided money for about 100 additional guards.

In attributing and getting to the 100 guards, half the lead is repeated. Slight recasting moves the story along:

Half of the Philadelphia Art Museum's permanent galleries were closed Sunday because the city had failed to provide money for 100 more security guards, Director Edward Turner said.

Attribute we must, but not necessarily in the lead. Sometimes the attribution can safely be deferred to the second paragraph or even later:

PHILADELPHIA—Former Defense Secretary Frank C. Carlucci has been elected to Bell Atlantic's board of directors, the telephone company announced.

WASHINGTON—The Catholic Archdiocese of Washington has announced that it will permanently close three of its four city high schools in June because of a decade-long decline in enrollment.

NEW ORLEANS—A week-long jazz festival is planned this summer in honor of the city's most famous brassman, Louis Armstrong, officials said.

By contrast, instant attribution was mandatory in the following lead. The writer couldn't be sure the secret talks had taken place:

SEOUL, South Korea—South Korea and North Korea have held secret talks on improving relations and discussed a possible meeting between their leaders, newspaper reports said today.

Horse First, Then Cart

Far too many leads start with long subsidiary clauses marching ahead of the main idea. That procedure usually delays the action. An additional reason for suspicion: You never hear that kind of a sentence in conversation.

Declaring that "a line has been drawn in the sand," President Bush announced yesterday a major deployment of U.S. military forces in Saudi Arabia. . .

In this instance, the introductory clause contains a striking phrase (which rarely happens) but even so, take the direct route:

President Bush warned Iraq yesterday that "a line has been drawn in the sand" as thousands of U.S. soldiers, sailors and airmen were dispatched to Saudi Arabia. . .

More commonly, the advance scout is limping:

Saying he is deeply bothered by reports of Superior Court officers leaving work early, the state's top administrative judge yesterday ordered an investigation into whether some of the officers are cheating the public out of a full day's work.

Let him mutter away and start with the action:

The state's top administrative judge yesterday ordered an investigation into reports that some court officers are cheating the public out of a full day's work.

Another example:

With consumers continuing their stay away from showrooms and the general economy showing further signs of decline, automakers today announced a new wave of layoffs in plants here and elsewhere.

The layoffs are the hard news:

Detroit automakers today announced new layoffs as car sales and the general economy continued to decline.

A short introductory phrase, on the other hand, is often effective:

One wing afire, an Air Force plane made a successful emergency landing at . . .

The test is simple: Does the phrase help what follows or just get in the way?

Another disruptive formula starts the lead with the subject, then meanders off into a dependent clause before getting to the verb and the news:

> President Bush, saying that relations with Mexico have never been better, will discuss trade matters with . . .

Often there's sound reason for starting a lead with the source, notably when the statement or action derives all its significance from the speaker or doer. Not much reason here:

> WASHINGTON —The General Accounting Office, an investigative branch of Congress, issued a report Tuesday recommending federal leadership . . .

Yes, yes, but what did it say?

> . . . to reduce the amount of low-level radioactive waste from nuclear plants.

Second-Cycle Woes

Overstuffing, double-decking and other fatal diseases are often encountered when the writer is struggling with that old nemesis, the second-cycle lead. Every reporter will eventually confront a second-cycle lead; for Associated Press reporters it is a part of the daily routine. Since phrases like "day before yesterday" are not in the vocabulary of leads, the problem arises in trying to make old news appear fresh. With no new development to come to the rescue, writers are left to their own resources.

Minimally, the second-cycle lead should cannibalize the first report for a different angle to stress.

An AMs story, for example, led with a bankruptcy judge's approval of $135 million in cash so Eastern Air Lines could keep flying through the winter. The PMs version led with a statement by the airline's trustee, which was subordinated in the original, that the cash infusion would be enough to help the carrier return to profitability.

The following second-day lead took a feature angle:

DILLINGHAM, Alaska—No matter how they voted in yesterday's election, some residents of the Bristol Bay region were sure to wind up with a turkey.

(A reward for the village with the highest turnout.)

And another fresh approach on the day after a fire:

UNIVERSAL CITY, Calif. (AP)—Hollywood tourists took a closeup look at a scene of destruction requiring no special effects: The gutting of the Universal Studios backlot.

Trams full of visitors rolled past smouldering remains . . .

This writer settled for the routine:

LAS VEGAS, Nev.—Arson investigators sifted through the rubble of a spectacular fire Sunday that leveled most of a shopping center just off the heart of the glittering Las Vegas strip.

The blaze that began Saturday night destroyed . . .

Leads that report investigators (or grim-faced rescue workers, or weary homeowners) *sifting through the rubble* or *poking through the debris* are written by writers wallowing in clichés. A narrative or anecdotal lead would be more interesting than those overworked rescue workers in disaster stories: *Most families in Smithtown were having supper when the sirens sounded. In the next few minutes. . .*

No fresh developments here, but the writer came up with an interesting angle by adding things up:

SAN RAFAEL, Calif.—The state of California spent 16 months and more than $2 million to convict three men who were already imprisoned, two with life sentences. Three of the San Quentin Six were found guilty Thursday . . .

That lead was written at the end of a trial. Reporters covering the early stages of a trial face tougher problems. Trials have moments of high drama, but the phase of jury selection is not among them. Yawning reporters often refer to it as the *long, tedious process* of seating a jury, but the process is far from tedious to lawyers and defendants, whose minds are on other matters than providing entertainment.

Terrible leads are often written during that phase: *Three more jurors were tentatively seated Thursday as the trial entered its fifth day*, which is later topped with a lead that has two more jurors chosen.

Obviously, the number of jurors chosen must be reported. Probably the best way to handle it is to mention high up that jury selection is continuing, and then, in the middle of your story, run a paragraph that by such and such a time X number of jurors had been picked. You can update the figures without changing the lead or breaking the continuity of the story. Meantime, work on a more interesting angle. For example:

> MINEOLA, N.Y. (AP)—Prospective jurors in the trial of a doctor charged with the "mercy killing" of a dying cancer patient were closely questioned about their religious beliefs and attitudes toward the medical profession.

This second-day lead makes a significant point. The numbers (*Eight jurors have been seated . . .*) fell into place later in the story.

Watch the Bouncing Ball

While on the subject of covering the courts, beware another snare in this special field of reporting. Court rulings, administrative decisions and the like are usually couched in technicalities and legalese, and leads don't always simplify these terms the way they should. Here's an example:

> A federal judge refused Wednesday to issue a temporary injunction halting a union ratification vote on the binding arbitration contract handed down last week for the American Postal Workers union and the U.S. Postal Service.

Anybody care to tell a struggling reader what happened? Well, it was like this. The judge wouldn't block the vote on a contract. Moreover, since the contract resulted from binding arbitration— meaning the union members weren't free to accept or reject it— the vote could have no effect. They were going through motions, that's all. So:

> A federal judge on Wednesday let postal workers go ahead with the formalities of voting on a new contract imposed through binding arbitration.

AP President and former Executive Editor Lou Boccardi calls this turgidity in court coverage "tennis-ball writing." Here's another example:

> WASHINGTON—The U.S. Court of Appeals agreed Wednesday to review a lower court order that found the Nuclear Regulatory Commission in contempt of court for violating an order to hold open budget meetings.

Boccardi's comment in his writing bulletin, *Prose and Cons*:
"The problem here is that we treat the reader's mind like a tennis ball to be whacked back and forth across the net. Agreed to review. Bam! Contempt of court. Bam! For violating an order. Bam! To hold open meetings. Bam! You can almost see the ball flying back and forth. It's just too much. You cure it by just stepping back and asking yourself, 'What really happened here?' " This happened:

> WASHINGTON—The U.S. Court of Appeals agreed Wednesday to review a contempt finding against the Nuclear Regulatory Commission for holding a closed meeting.

Reporters indulge in tennis-ball writing and legal jargon because they don't quite trust themselves to tell in a straightforward way what's going on. By sticking to the legal terms, they play it safe. Here's an example of playing it so safe the story is unintelligible:

> RICHMOND, Va.—Attorney General Andrew P. Miller says a juvenile who in a juvenile or domestic relations court is convicted of and receives a sentence for what, if committed by an adult, would be a misdemeanor or a felony cannot be housed with adult prisoners in prisons or jails.
>
> In an opinion released Monday, Miller said it would be a violation of state law to incarcerate juveniles in such a manner unless the incarceration is mainly for the purpose of pre-trial detention or if the juvenile is certified to a circuit court and tried as an adult.

That's a legal tennis match to boggle the mind. In English, I presume it would mean this:

> RICHMOND, Va.—A youthful offender receiving a prison sentence in a juvenile or domestic relations court cannot be jailed with adult prisoners, the attorney general has ruled.

Placing him with adult inmates would violate state law unless it's for pre-trial detention or he's been tried in a circuit court.

Legalistic Leads

In covering police and court stories, there is sometimes legitimate use in the lead for otherwise cumbersome or legalistic words and phrases. One of these is *in connection with* in stories about people who are questioned or arrested or sought for a crime with which they haven't been charged. But there's absolutely no warrant for using it *after* a man has been charged (say what he was charged with) or after he's been sentenced or pronounced guilty. Some reporters are so afflicted with the legal shakes that you can read:

Joseph Smith was scheduled Monday to be sentenced in connection with the Smithtown murder after a jury convicted him . . .

Another abused word is *suspect*. It's seldom a very good word to use in any case; if somebody's questioned, or wanted for questioning, let those facts speak for themselves. If the authorities declare somebody to be *a prime suspect* in a case, so be it; quote them. It is ridiculous in crime stories, however, to refer to unknown but indubitable culprits as *suspects*. While nobody knows their names, they're the ones who have done it:

Two suspects held up a jewelry store at 14th and Main today, tying up a clerk and rifling several display cases before escaping.

The Time Element

A special problem with leads is comparatively recent: the shift to the use of the day of the week. *Today* and *yesterday* fit gracefully into leads. Thursday and Friday are often balky.

As a rule, put the time element after the verb unless the day of the week can be read as the object of the verb or is awkward in other ways, producing oddities. A Washington story reports that Congress *postponed Wednesday*. In New York, a top federal mediator *sought Thursday*, presumably without finding it. A story begins, *Middlesex Superior Court Judge Henry Chielinsky Thursday. . .*

Some writers stick *on* before the day, interrupting the succession of capital letters, but this is generally considered a non-solution, adding a word with little gain.

There's no ready formula. You must use your ear as well as your eye. How does it sound? Some leads read well with the day of the week, others don't. When it's cumbersome no matter where you try to shoehorn the word into a sentence, drop the day to the second paragraph, where it often fits quite naturally. You do *not* have to put the time element in every lead, either AMs or PMs.

Wrestling with such small details, and with many larger matters of technique, may be joyless, but in leads every word must count. Some of my editing of clumsy leads cited earlier doubtless could be improved further. The direction in any case should be clear: Toward a lean, uncluttered sentence, toward the news itself rather than byplay, toward logical order of thought, toward concrete and specific language. Those are the lead writer's goals.

THE CASE FOR THE PERIOD

4

Sentences come under special strains in news writing. A lot of facts have to be squeezed into tight space; afterthoughts are often accommodated in haste. There's a tendency to overload sentences and let them swell to unseemly length.

But the longer the sentence, the less readable it's likely to be, the more exposed to mishaps of syntax. The remedy is simple: Chop up long sentences into their functional components and aim for an average sentence length of 16 to 17 words.

Note that I say "average." We don't want all sentences to be that short; you'd be writing kindergarten stuff. But the average gives you leeway for a comely mixture; let short sentences predominate, relieved by occasional longer sentences. Variety of sentence structure further insures against monotony.

There are no absolute rules of good writing—generalizations are instantly riddled with exceptions—but the principle of the 16-word average comes closest. No other single step you can take will show such quick results in clarity and vigor.

Short sentences are not for everyone. They worked splendidly for Hemingway, as they work for Annie Dillard today. They worked for the James Joyce of *Dubliners*—never mind *Finnegans Wake*—but you won't find many in Melville or Faulkner.

It's not necessary that every passage in every story meet the brevity standard, though all stories should approximate it as a whole. Whenever the average climbs to 20 and above, many readers are in trouble.

Long, complicated sentences present no obstacle to professional readers (like ourselves). But we don't write for professional readers. And even they prefer the tighter prose that a preponderance of short, declarative sentences creates.

The bright side to the obesity syndrome is that it's so simple to control. The period mark in lieu of all those conjunctions, participial and relative clauses is a splendid antidote. Some of us need to rediscover it.

First aid, not major surgery, is usually all that's needed. Let's see how it works with sentences of the kind that often lure writers into quicksand.

A good way to deflate sentences stuffed with relative clauses is to use pronouns whenever they offer a smooth alternative.

Cabinet ministers, leading politicians and foreign envoys were caught up in the melee that erupted moments after President Daniel arap Moi left the grounds of the Valley Road Pentecostal Church in his official limousine.

Thousands of people had gathered outside the church, about a mile from downtown Nairobi, for the service of Robert Ouko, whose charred body was found with a bullet hole through the skull near his farm in western Kenya on Feb. 16.

Break up those sentences of 34 and 41 words and you come up with 13, 20, 20 and 21:

Cabinet ministers, leading politicians and foreign envoys were caught up in the melee. It erupted moments after President Daniel arap Moi left the grounds of the Valley Road Pentecostal Church in his limousine.

Thousands of people had gathered outside the church, about a mile from downtown Nairobi, for the service for Robert Ouko. His charred body was found with a bullet hole through his skull near his farm in western Kenya on Feb. 16.

Sentences can often be shortened by getting rid of dependent clauses starting with "although," "even though," etc.

But the commission led by Moakley said Wednesday that doubts remain as to whether the people who planned the slayings have been identified, even though a Salvadoran army colonel has been arrested.

Turn this around (and forget "as to whether"):

A Salvadoran army colonel has been arrested. But the commission led by Moakley said Wednesday it's doubtful that the people who planned the slayings have been identified.

Avoid pointless prepositional phrases:

Cheney said some 5,000 of the troops would be pulled out of South Korea, with an additional 7,000 to 9,400 being withdrawn from the Philippines, officials said.

Two sentences:

Cheney said some 5,000 of the troops would be pulled out of South Korea. An additional 7,000 to 9,400 would be withdrawn from the Philippines, officials said.

Guard against long dependent clauses and appositives:

Those transfers, estimated by Selma's two all-white private schools to be as many as 35 in one day, included the sixth-grade son of white school board member Edie Jones, who enrolled Monday at all-white Morgan Academy in Selma.

That's 41 words. The underlined words are superfluous in the context. But let's unravel:

Selma's two all-white private schools estimate that those transfers could have reached 35 in one day. One youngster, who enrolled in the sixth grade at Morgan Academy Monday, is the son of white school board member Edie Jones.

We now have 17 and 20, respectively.
The next sentence, 35 words, cries out for a strategic period mark and slight rephrasing:

But they said they would not attend classes as they pursued their demands for the retention of the city's first black superintendent, and for the placement of more black students in higher-level courses.

A more manageable version at 20 and 10:

But they said they would skip classes to pursue their demands for retention of the city's first black school superintendent. They also want more black students in higher-level courses.

Next is a slightly different type of heavyweight, 39 words:

The young Soviet state under Lenin's leadership confiscated most private property after the 1917 revolution and Stalin's drive to strip peasants of their land through collectivization in the 1930s claimed millions of lives through famine, deportation and summary execution.

You have two long independent clauses linked by a conjunction. Cut the link:

The young Soviet state under Lenin's leadership confiscated private property after the 1917 revolution. Later, Stalin's drive to strip peasants of their land through collectivization in the early 1930s claimed millions of lives through famine, deportation and summary execution.

Similar surgery in the following lead:

WASHINGTON (AP)—Federal Reserve Chairman Alan Greenspan said today the economy has likely passed the danger point for an imminent recession, and he predicted continued, although modest, economic growth for the rest of this year.

End it after "recession" and carry on with "He predicted continued . . . " etc.

The next example is a somewhat messy lead; again two independent clauses glued together with a conjunction:

NEW YORK (AP)—Cable TV mogul Ted Turner urged advertisers to take the high road and keep in mind long-term interests in programs they sponsor, and accused the three largest networks of being more concerned with audience size than quality.

Substitute a pronoun for the second "and":

NEW YORK (AP)—Cable TV mogul Ted Turner urged advertisers to take the high road and keep in mind long-term interests in the programs they sponsor. He accused the three largest networks of being more concerned with size than quality.

This is still a bit much for a lead but at least it's two sentences of 24 and 15 words each rather than one 38-word gulp.

When, after, as and similar crutches often prolong sentences needlessly:

The company will not issue a general recall in its home country after a preliminary ruling by Health Ministry officials that it poses no public danger, Levin said.

Why not simply:

The company will not issue a general recall in its home country. A preliminary ruling by Health Ministry officials found no danger to the public, Levin said.

Obviously the ruling preceded the decision.

CHRISTOPHER, Ill. (AP)—The long-distance courtship of Toby the robot by an infatuated doll named Jodi ended just before Valentine's Day when Toby learned that Jodi had gone to the big doll house in the sky.

This good lead becomes crisper by deleting the "when":

CHRISTOPHER, Ill. (AP)—The long-distance courtship of Toby the robot by an infatuated doll named Jodi ended just before Valentine's Day. Toby learned that Jodi had gone to the big doll house in the sky.

This sentence achieves 49 words:

"U.S. troops will remain in Korea as long as they are needed to guarantee the peace, and the Korean and American peoples and governments want them to remain," Cheney said after arriving from Hawaii on the first stop of a two-week tour of Asian nations hosting the U.S. forces.

Period after "Cheney said." "He arrived from Hawaii," etc.

This 34-word graf is strengthened by dropping the conjunction.

While talks on reunification opened, another piece of the Cold War headed into oblivion as East German border guards started dismantling the Berlin Wall between the Reichstag building and the Checkpoint Charlie border crossing.

The initial "while" establishes the sequence; the "as" merely blunts the sentence.

While talks on reunification opened, another piece of the Cold War headed into oblivion. East German border guards started dismantling the Berlin Wall between the Reichstag building and the Checkpoint Charlie border crossing.

We're too fond of participial phrases that merely lengthen sentences and slow the pace:

The civil rights groups' national chairman, William F. Gibson of Greenville, S.C., announced the agreement with the Columbia Mall on Monday, saying it was the first pact reached with a shopping mall on the hiring and treatment of blacks.

That's 38 words. Period after "Monday," and "He said . . ."

The following graf from a Jerusalem story is weighed down by 45 words:

Peres was responding to Likud's decision earlier in the day to seek guarantees that left-leaning Labor stands united with Likud in peace talks, refusing any PLO involvement in the negotiations or any step that would hint at Israel relinquishing control of Arab east Jerusalem.

Easily tamed with a period and slight rephrasing:

Peres was responding to Likud's decision earlier in the day to seek guarantees that left-leaning Labor stands united with Likud in peace talks. That means refusing any PLO involvement in the negotiations or any step at Israel's relinquishing control of Arab east Jerusalem.

Here's a routine bit of narrative, the sort where individual sentences usually spread like the oil slick they describe—readably, because the sentence average is 15 words.

When the leak stopped Thursday night, the Coast Guard began pumping the remaining oil and water from the compartment onto a barge. By 6 a.m. today, about 26,000 gallons had been transferred, said Lt. Cmdr. Alan Carver.

Ten skimming boats worked on the slick, which covered water over an area roughly measuring 6 miles by 4 miles. Seas were calm and winds light.

"The weather has cooperated," Carver said.

Offshore winds Thursday had kept the slick away from beaches until afternoon, when they reversed direction and began nudging the mess onto shore. Pockets of crude oil began washing ashore Thursday night.

A 4-mile stretch was fouled in Newport Beach, an affluent community that boasts some of Southern California's most expensive beachfront property.

That's how we write in our simple-and-direct mode, avoiding entanglements and convulsions. And it's the practice wherever clarity and readability are cherished.

That much-admired British weekly, *The Economist*, deals with heavy subjects; the writing is light and bright. Many intros average 16 words. Much of the copy hovers between 16 and 19, usually at the low end of the scale. *The Economist* is not written for dummies.

JOURNALESE

5

Like the character from a Molière play who was astounded to learn that he'd been speaking prose all his life, many news writers might be surprised to hear that much of the time they're writing journalese.

One would like to say that this sub-language is bush-league stuff, manufactured by raw novices at backwater weeklies. One would like to say it, but it isn't true.

Hardly any news organization is entirely free of the contagion, and even polished writers and prestigious publications will lapse occasionally. Nor can we blame invading bureaucratese and alien jargons. Journalese is our very own. The bacteria are nurtured in our professional culture. This enemy of sophisticated tone is us.

The plague goes back to the fossil strata of the profession, the era of drinkers and wanderers who loved to whoop it up and make great noise in their copy as in their lives, and didn't mind stretching a fact or two.

Those wild days are gone, but journalese still flourishes. New—if instantly old—terms have been added (*send a message, target, charisma*), but much of the old stock vocabulary remains in use (*crucial, ironic, historic, unique*).

It was about 30 years ago when Wilson Follett, in his *Modern American Usage*, explained the phenomenon:

"In general, journalese is the tone of contrived excitement," he wrote. "When the facts by themselves do not make the reader's pulse beat faster, the journalist thinks it is his duty to apply the spur and whip of breathless phrases. Since these exist only in finite numbers they get repeated, and repetition begets their weakening, their descent into journalese."

This underworld bears some examination for its power to transform gold into plastic by reverse alchemy.

Let's assume two ordinary mortals, neighbors, are discussing a recent disturbance in their suburb, and run their conversation through this process:

SMITH: Joe, I'll note candidly that my concern has been escalating for weeks, and the latest incident has really fueled my ire. What's triggering our area youths, who keep sparking confrontations down by our tranquil duck pond?

JONES: They certainly shattered the stillness of the affluent neighborhood with their drug-related pre-dawn rampage. No wonder violence flared when the club-wielding police reached the turbulent scene. I understand the Doe youth had to be rushed to a nearby medical facility.

SMITH: Yes, he is lingering in guarded condition. His mother is grief-stricken. But I am thankful that our usually soft-spoken, mild-mannered, pipe-puffing—not to say wimpy—mayor lashed out at the alleged suspects, vowing to curb future outbursts.

JONES: He certainly fired off a clear signal. His move spawns some hope of resolving the problem.

This exchange doesn't exactly throb with the vigor of the American idiom. Nobody talks that way. But that's how news is too often written—in smaller blotches, true, but enough to drain the life from many a story.

Take the following passage:

The president, whose wavering stance on the question of boosting taxes on the rich has sparked frustration and ridicule on Capitol Hill, has expressed confidence that a plan will be hammered together.

News copy isn't written for the ages, but this sentence has a shelf life of two seconds. It's mechanically "hammered together" from prefabricated phrases. Almost any version in plain English will be better:

The president's waffling over tax increases for the rich has stirred up annoyance and ridicule on Capitol Hill, but he says he is confident that something will be worked out.

The next example sounds like my parody:

The 700-member union struck *The Daily News* last night, triggering a climactic labor confrontation with the management of the financially ailing paper.

Less shrill:

The 700-member union struck *The Daily News* last night for the final showdown in a long, bitter labor dispute with the management of the paper. *The News* has been losing money for years.

None of this is extreme. You can pluck examples at random every day:

Tensions mounted in Israel as the Gulf crisis escalated . . .

Tensions between Arizona's two senators flared before the Senate's ethics committee . . .
(Arizona's two senators quarreled openly before the Senate ethics committee . . .)

In a move aimed at increasing revenues, the airline is hiking its full coach fares—the unrestricted, widely available fares targeted toward business travelers.
(Trying to increase revenues, the airline is raising its full coach fares—unrestricted, widely available fares intended for business travelers.)

An immediate focus of concern is the United States' intention to break off dialogue . . .
(An immediate worry is the United States' intention to break off talks . . .)

President Mikhail Gorbachev yesterday won the Nobel Peace Prize for easing international tensions . . .
(for helping to end the Cold War . . .)

The thorny issue of free agency was brought into sharper focus . . .
(. . . received fresh attention . . .)

A more elaborate example is the following story. It's dramatic and clearly told, but for journalese enough is never enough:

A *blazing* fire broke out on the 47th floor of a Lower Manhattan sky-scraper today, threatening to turn it into a *towering inferno*.

Seven persons were injured—at least one critically—and two others were reported missing, the Fire Department said.

Hundreds—many of whom had been eating in a *posh* restaurant—fled the building.

Traffic on Lower Broadway was brought to a *complete* halt.

An unidentified cleaning man who was riding the freight elevator was injured when the elevator opened on the 47th floor.

Flames *exploded* and *blasted* him in the face.

"His body was ignited head to foot," a witness said.

The fire is *blazing*, the restaurant *posh*, traffic doesn't just come to a halt but a *complete* halt, flames explode *and* blast and ignite the man from head to foot. (And where was the witness? In the *inferno*, clad in asbestos?)

Enough journalese slides into news copy to multiply examples without great effort. We can quarrel over a word here and there and disagree whether a given context supports a supercharged term. But I doubt that there's much argument about the underlying distemper, those breathless words and phrases; the compulsion, for instance, to "ignite" a "wrenching debate" in Poland's presidential campaign because "wrenching" without ignition wouldn't be strong enough.

Writers of journalese chain themselves to the particular catchwords and clichés of their dialect. Explosions (always violent) must rip, earthquakes endlessly rock, spectacular fires sweep—often trapping victims as horrified spectactors stand by helplessly. Later, grim-faced rescue workers comb through smoldering rubble to the wails of grief-stricken relatives.

Politicians *lambaste, assail, rap,* or *lash out at*; otherwise they *craft legislation, policies,* or *strategies.* Often they *vow*, never merely *promise, pledge,* or *say.*

Police are *club-wielding*, assailants *knife-wielding*, troops *heavily armed*. Tempers, tensions, violence all *flare* (sometimes, embarrassingly, spelled *flair*). Dissidents *stalk*, never *walk*, from halls. Demonstrators *spark angry confrontations*. Rain doesn't fall but is *dumped* as rivers *rampage*.

Prices are *hiked* or *boosted*, hopes or enterprises are *spawned* (never mind that the verb relates to fish eggs) and nothing merely *starts, is created* or *quickened;* things are *triggered, sparked* and *fueled.* In journalese, you can even read about a "chilling effect fueled by the court decision" in a libel case.

Heads of state and other august public figures may still be hailed, as Julius Caesar was, but no longer do they *warn, hint, suggest* or *imply.* The secretary of state's speech *sends a message.* The White House *emits signals—clear, strong* or *mixed.* Egypt's president "signals the alarm of Arab countries with a surprise visit to two of them." ("Surprise" usually signals a reporter's failure to get advance word.) When prosecutors indict the physician-inventor of a suicide machine, they do it to "send a clear message" to other would-be facilitators.

But why go on with the kind of stuff you'll be reading—but I hope not writing—tomorrow? Still, two more words, each used as verb and noun, deserve mention because they are so lavishly overused: *called for* and *concern(ed).* They've been turned into dimwitted predators, nosing into places where other, more specific words would serve better or at least offer relief from monotony.

President Bush calls for a budget compromise. The senator called on the two agencies to settle their feud. The administration bill calls for major revisions. All but forgotten in this unseemly bellowing are *urged, recommended, proposed, suggested, asked for, demanded, requested,* among others.

Not surprisingly, a check of just the AP's national report for three weeks turned up "called for" and slight variants 347 times. Project that over a year, and you get nearly 10,000. Add newspapers' own usage, and we may reach 15,000 or more. That's overloading.

"Concern," "concerned," "express concern" are in wide general use and not typically journalese except for the overpowering monomania that expects a single bass fiddle to cover the range of an orchestra. It may be *the* word-of-all-trades, showing up 543 times in three weeks on the AP news report. Consider these examples:

The Israelis have expressed concern (are worried) that a unified Germany would dominate Europe.

City hall now is seriously concerned (alarmed) by the wave of killings.

Soviet citizens now are more concerned with (interested in) their own economy.

He was concerned about (sympathetic to) his aide's plight.

The board refused because it was concerned about (objected to) taking on more debt.

The community is determined to address the AIDS patients' concerns (determined to meet the AIDS patients' needs).

When one general term eclipses so many meanings, precision is lost, and this is one way in which journalese sets its traps for the unwary and the negligent. Competent writers manage to avoid them, and it is they who account for the genuine quality of much of our journalism.

The following story, on Yugoslavia's travail, offers an example. The writer might have trotted out the shopworn standbys. He might have talked of "escalating confrontations," of "rising tensions throughout the embattled country," of "acute crises in the republics," and so on. You'll find none of that in this intro to a *New York Times* story—only specifics reported in vivid but never overdrawn language.

BELGRADE, Yugoslavia—Intensifying conflicts and rivalries among Yugoslavia's republics are bringing the country dangerously close to the breaking point, say people who favor the process as well as those who fear it.

Nerves are fraying throughout the country. In Slovenia, the Government has deployed its own armed guards to underscore claims that the republic's sovereignty is paramount. In Croatia, gangs of heavily-armed Serbs have blocked roads in the enclaves where they are numerically strong. In Serbia's Kosovo region, ethnic Albanians speak openly of armed uprising. Travel from republic to republic, and the inventory of conflict grows.

An international effort may soon be needed to head off a conflagration, Slovenia's Prime Minister, Lojze Peterie, said this week.

A dream of 19th-century Slav Romantics, Yugoslavia is now a crumbling mosaic of peoples of Eastern Orthodox, Roman Catholic or Muslim traditions who have lived since World War II in a federation.

Though conflicts and vendettas laced the region for years, for much of the postwar period national unity was advanced by a modicum of prosperity and the now-defunct Yugoslav Communist Party's monopoly, which muffled the quarrels.

Much like the erosion of central power and rise of nationalist emotions in the Soviet Union, the breakdown of Communist-imposed unity and the emergence of democratic openness in Yugoslavia have released long-suppressed national aspirations, envies and antagonisms.

This is sober, effective news writing, without trumpets blaring, metaphors clashing and harlequins yodeling. The words both tell and show, and there's never a shriek.

Journalese in its overemphatic mode is like the great dane that's never outgrown its puppyhood and leaps up at his owner's cringing guests to beslobber their faces. It's a way to get attention, but not the best.

Even more coldly put, journalese means hack work. To write well means to choose the right words for each occasion, not to fit the occasion to precooked words. That requires a thoughtful effort. And as Samuel Johnson said long ago, "What is written without effort is in general read without pleasure."

TONE:
The Inner
Music of Words
6

After you've squared away your lead, herded your paragraphs into place, and swept up the small verbal debris, lend an ear. Does your copy sound conversational or stilted? Pompous or overly breezy? Formal or relaxed?

Tone ultimately determines whether your reader is pleased or not. Sentence structure has something to do with it, but tone is primarily generated by the choice of words. Plain, short, familiar words produce one distinct tone; fancy polysyllables another.

And then there are the "insides" of words. Many words have a special inner music—clusters of associations and images that lurk just below the surface.

House, home, residence and *domicile* all denote the same thing, but only a tone-deaf writer (which should be a contradiction in terms) would use them interchangeably, regardless of context. *The old couple lived in a cozy residence* rings false; but there's nothing wrong with *they changed their residence frequently.*

Emulate, copy and *ape* refer to the same activity, but you wouldn't write that a worthy novice was *aping* a saint. You'd use *emulate*, because it has honorable connotations, while *copy* suggests a mindless, mechanical process and *ape* has contemptuous overtones.

A word utterly misused destroys tone with a primal scream:

The executive finally conceded to his transfer (consented to).

61

But authorities said that the flight delays that wrenched thousands of travelers over the Thanksgiving weekend should ease. . . .

Not even the airlines can wrench you.
Most questions of tone are subtler. Consider these passages:

But long-term positive aspects of the revolutionary process far transcended initial defects. The American Revolution was dynamic, not static, and took it upon itself to amend and improve imperfections in its structure.

When George Bush's people took Sen. Sam Nunn aside at the end of 1988 and whispered in his ear that a job as defense secretary might be an offer, he told them not to bother. Mr. Nunn reckoned that, as chairman of the Senate Armed Services Committee, he already had as much say in matters of war and peace as he would get at the Pentagon. And after all, he said, he was a Democrat.

The first passage is from a newspaper, the second from a magazine. Both passages deal with serious subjects and both are clear, but they are octaves apart in tone. One is weighed down by ponderous abstract words of a distinctly academic flavor; you might say it's static, not dynamic. The other is almost conversational, skipping along on plain words and homely analogies.

Avoid Sudden Shifts

Tone need not be uniform, but sudden shifts are disconcerting, and a mixture of disparate tones grates like chalk on a slate.
Charles Dickens makes use of this effect with his immortal Mr. Micawber, whose passion for ornate language is happily tempered by his impulse to self-correction:

Under the impression that your peregrinations in this Metropolis have not yet been extensive, and you might have difficulty in penetrating the arena of the modern Babylon . . . *In short, that you might get lost* . . .

Again and again Mr. Micawber, soaring, abruptly pulls himself back to earth. That's the side of him news writers should emulate.
Tone can go wrong in many ways besides turning pompous. It can, for example, become gushy, like the language you find in much advertising and promotion copy, in certain magazines and newspaper sections.

Words that usually signal gush are many, including *fabulous, tremendous, superb, unique, exquisite, gorgeous, fantastic, enchanting, incredible, glamorous* and the like. Public relations handouts are often gushers, and too much of that breathless verbiage slips through:

> Officials of the cable company said the *long-awaited* unveiling of the system will occur June 27, *ushering in a fabulous new viewing era.* . . .

The system will start operation June 27 says it all.

> The ship is *posh* from stem to stern, a floating *lap of luxury*, with *exquisite* food and a whirl of activities that keeps cruise passengers *tingling.*

It must be uncomfortable to float in a lapful of luxury, fabulous or otherwise. No wonder the passengers tingle.

A gushy lead:

> There's something special about rivers, those winding and weaving waterways that just flow on and on. Lakes are lovely. Ponds are pleasant. But there's something about them—they just aren't rivers.

A New York critic starts a review this way:

> Excitement twinkled in the air like champagne bubbles in a spotlight. . .

Which seems a good spot to stop reading.

We Are Not Amused

Never treat death, pain and suffering—human or animal—lightly or humorously. The following story takes a persistently wrong tone:

So, you think you've got problems? Wait till you hear the story of Chuh-Chuh, the shih-tzu from Howard Beach.

Sour Note 1: The lead asks the reader to identify with a dog.

The dog's owners filed for $5.1 million damages yesterday in state Supreme Court, claiming they had suffered distress and

Sour Note 2: Details of animal's suffering and owners' grief make flippant lead doubly dubious.

psychological pain, while the dog suffered prolonged pain following castration by a veterinarian. Chuh-Chuh died in early August, nine days after the operation.

The veterinarian said the owner's attorney, Harry L. Lipsig, had a bark that is worse than his bite. Dr. Donald Wirth of the Lefferts Dog and Cat Hospital denied that he was responsible for the death of Chuh-Chuh.

Sour Note 3: More limp flippancy. Did the vet really say that?

"What the hell are they suing me for?" he said. "A lot of people have strong attachments to their pets. But this is outrageous. Shih-tzus are nice little dogs that cost about $300."

Sour Note 4: "'What the hell" quote is pointless.

Lipsig said, "There is the pain and suffering the poor creature went through. He was practically a member of the family."

Some readers might be amused by this treatment, but a great many more would put on a long face.

Few readers would chuckle over the lead to a story that police officers had "loads of trouble" recovering the body of a circus worker crushed by an elephant that fell on him.

Less flagrant but still the wrong tone:

Mister Donut of America is suing a franchise holder for breach of contract, saying a police raid at the shop that uncovered crack cocaine and stolen property has left holes in the company's reputation.

I doubt that the company put it that way or that grins are in order here.

For reasons of tone, likewise, don't refer to serious accidents as *mishaps*. A man twisting his ankle stepping off a curb has a mishap; if a car hits him and he's paralyzed from the waist down, it's an accident. The word *incident* also suggests something of small consequence, a peripheral event—say a picket line scuffle. A shootout in which several are hurt or killed is more than an *incident*.

Beware the Personal Touch

Addressing readers directly makes for a pleasantly personal tone in stories that lend themselves to this approach. But beware of casting readers in roles they can't readily envision for themselves, and don't link them to something disagreeable, as the lead of the dog story did.

If you've ever struggled with a garden full of weeds is a situation ordinary enough so that readers, non-gardeners included, have no trouble seeing themselves that way. But when you write, *If you've ever thought about biting the head off a live chicken*, the personal note turns bizarre and the reader's response will be muted at best.

The following lead is lively and clever in that it mimics the writing style of the subject, a book author. But unless you are aware of that, it demands too much willingness to pretend:

> NEW YORK—You are practicing law in New York, supporting a family and paying the bills. But in your spare time, you are also writing children's books—in longhand, in your battered spiral notebook.
>
> What do you do? If you choose to remain a lawyer, this is the end of your story. But if you are Edward Packard, you chuck the law career. . . .

Somewhere soon in this list of particulars, the *you* is apt to stir uneasily and ask, *Who, me?*

Don't Be Absurd

The writer of the following passage is flirting with absurdity from the start and finally embraces it. The story concerned a sex education program for the very, very young. The exuberant tone adds to the difficulty of keeping a straight face:

> The child picked up the plastic model of a uterus, examined it closely and announced: "This looks like a frog."
>
> The resemblance was remote, but his parents were nonetheless happy. They had begun a dialogue with their 3-year-old son that they hoped would continue through his childhood and adolescence.

The tone shuttles between the pompous and the cutesy and collapses with the unlikely suggestion of a serious dialogue with a 3-year-old.

Since the writer intended readers to take the project seriously, he would have done better to flatten out the passage, perhaps like this:

> The child picked up the plastic uterus and said it looked like a frog. For the parents, it was the start of teaching their 3-year-old something about the facts of life. They want him to continue to discuss the subject with them freely through childhood and adolescence.

A far more subtle example is offered by a fine story that has perfect pitch except for two notes slightly off key. The writer is telling it through the youngsters' experiences, and the simple style is in tune and rhythm:

> When 10-year-old Midaglia Roman learned that she wasn't promoted with her fourth grade class this year, she cried all the way home.

> Today, Midaglia got her second chance. "I'd rather be here," the pretty, big-eyed girl said as she sat with about 30 others in a warm classroom at Public School 34, where the Board of Education is running a special summer school for students who were "left back" under a get-tough policy.

The story continues in this vein until:

> Many, like Midaglia, will have a final try at the reading test when it's given again Aug. 14. They hope to *hone their skills* sufficiently in the coming week so they can go on with their class.

And in a later paragraph:

> But some students were less happy about the *intrusion on their summer plans.*

This story reads well as it stands. But the writer has been so attentive to keeping the tone modulated to youngsters' ways of thinking that the phrases *honed their skills* and *intrusion on their summer plans* add a sudden touch of stuffiness. *Brush up on their reading* and *missing out on some summer fun* might have been more consistent.

Dealing with Motive

Such nuances belong to the upper reaches of feature writing, perhaps. But dealing with motives is another matter, and can be a problem in straight news.

It's tricky because, for one thing, you can't be sure of a person's motive unless you're a mind reader. And second, a person's motives are often mixed.

So it needs delicate handling. That wasn't done in a story that had a governor, believed to be primping for a Senate race, "apparently courting the Jewish vote as he attacked the planned sale of $8.5 billion in arms to Saudi Arabia."

As AP President Lou Boccardi once commented in a note to the staff:

"We can't be so naive that we think governors speak without considering the political effects of what they say. But we also can't say the man is simply appealing for votes rather than expressing views truly held. It's clumsy and does him a disservice."

Better, but still wide of the mark:

AUSTIN, Texas—Land Commissioner Bob Armstrong announced the "good news" today that the Permanent School fund had reached $3 billion, then admitted he was thinking about running for governor.

The writer doesn't say so outright, but the tone is unmistakable and the announcement is linked to political motive.

It was done correctly in two stories where a news subject's special interests were mentioned as legitimate background without directly linking them to their statements.

One concerned a speech by the sponsor of a bill to relax air pollution standards. He argued that the best way to clean up the air was to encourage people to junk their old cars and buy new ones.

Only after he had had his say, farther down in the story came a mention that the congressman represented a district where the auto industry was dominant.

Similarly, the fact that a congressman who spoke out against military-base closings came from a district that would be directly affected was mentioned in the story—but not in the lead that dealt with his speech.

In other words, no winks, leers, or nudges, just the objective background.

No Hints, Please

Matters of tone and motive loom large also in investigative stories where writers sometimes resort to hints and innuendoes and suggestive arrangements of damaging detail to establish what the evidence itself fails to demonstrate:

> *Incredibly,* Smith did not report his failure to file the returns until eight long years later.

> In another of those *remarkable "coincidences,"* the records were damaged by a *convenient* fire four days before the subpoena arrived. *Of course* the defendants claimed they hadn't known the records were being sought.

> The young prosecutor said *candidly* he had all but given up on the case. Doe, asked about the turn of events, withdrew once again into a *sullen* "no comment."

This tone is editorial, snide and, in essence, prosecutorial. And, paradoxically, it is usually much less effective than factual, detached statement. If you have solid information logically marshaled, the readers will draw their own inferences, without the aid of zingers.

They will be more readily persuaded the less you resort to emotive words, small injections of opinion, knowing winks and lopsided selection of details. The less you comment or characterize, the better. An obvious attempt to push readers toward a foreshadowed conclusion is self-defeating; many resist such ham-handed pressure tactics. And, of course, there's the matter of objectivity, as crucial in investigative as any other form of reporting.

Perhaps there's a mindset to investigative reporting that sometimes betrays writers into the prosecutorial tone. Gene Roberts, who retired in 1990 as executive editor of the *Philadelphia Inquirer*—which has a notable record of major investigative projects—touched on the subject in a discussion at an Associated Press Managing Editors convention.

"I think where many papers go astray in trying to do alleged investigative reporting is in defining it as unearthing criminals," he said. "This immediately casts the reporters as cops rather than as gatherers of information. Society will get along quite well without newsrooms that view themselves as police forces."

Roberts doesn't even like the word *investigative*, and on the *Inquirer* "we stay away from the term 'investigative stories' in favor of terms like 'takeouts' and 'project pieces.'"

He added, "The finest reporting, short or long, is always investigative in that it digs and digs and digs. The finest writing is almost by definition explanatory in that it puts things so vividly, so compellingly, that readers see and understand."

Watch It, Kiddo

An informal, relaxed tone appeals to most people, but avoid excessive colloquialism and forced heartiness; don't get too chummy with your readers. It's an affectation and a form of writing down:

> The board of directors, after a daylong wrangle, lowered the boom on Smith. He was the third top honcho of the corporation to get the ax in as many years.

This is painful stuff, not because it offends the majesty of a corporation, but because backslapping breeziness has no place in a serious story.

A story retelling some of Iran's turbulent history also hits wrong keys:

> The late Shah, who *got kicked out* of the country in . . .
>
> But he was forced into wandering when country after country *sent him packing.*

And similarly, an anniversary piece on the Russian revolution recalled that:

> In 1917, when the czar *got the boot* . . .

A czar is forced from his throne, not booted or fired. Besides, this czar got more than the boot—the Communists, in a famous euphemism, dismissed him with extreme prejudice. He was shot.

Referring to news subjects by first name also carries informality too far. It's most often practiced on entertainment figures, athletes and other celebrities. The reporter is showing off a familiarity that's usually spurious, and the reader senses it.

It's different in writing about youngsters, when the use of the last name seems forced—up to age 15, anyway. Consistent use of the first name sounds more natural here. (However, if your lad has committed some ghastly, adult crimes, I would drop the first-name basis for obvious reasons.) And avoid references like *the Jones boy* or *the Smith woman*, which are simply rude.

Euphemism: Use and Misuse

With all cultural indicators in our society pointing to the more explicit, "genteelism"—the refined tone that dotes on overly polite words and euphemisms—has been fading from daily journalism, though it still survives.

It survives in part because of jargon, which has invaded all parts of the language and among other defacements substitutes abstractions and euphemism for plain words: *disadvantaged* for the poor, *underachievers* for the lazy or unwilling or downright mean, *senior citizens* for the elderly or old, *interact* for mingle with or make friends, *disturbed* for the mentally ill or violent, and many more.

Blather imported from the social sciences is a rich tributary to this variant of genteelism. Government is another fertile source. A fine example bowing in lately is *revenue enhancement*, much more agreeable than *tax increase*.

Other genteelisms, best avoided, are *mortician* for undertaker, *interment* for burial, *casket* for coffin, *lady* for woman, and *expecting* for pregnant. Even *pass away* for die still survives, and one Midwestern paper in a wedding story had the couple *motoring to their honeymoon haven*, a delightful archaism and most genteel.

All this is not to rule out euphemism entirely. We use it legitimately to avoid vulgarity or to soften something innately disgusting. Unlike genteelism, that is genuine politeness to the reader. As Theodore Bernstein mildly put it in *The Careful Writer*, "It may be preferable to write that a man and a woman 'spent the night together' than to set forth in detail how they spent it."

Euphemism is objectionable only when used to doll up an emotionally stark but otherwise unexceptional fact of the human condition.

There's a directly musical aspect of tone that also deserves attention in news writing—those inadvertent collisions of syllables

and sounds that cause readers pause (as cause/pause does in this
sentence). A string of words ending in *'shun*, for example, grates:
*The organization gave attention to the situation. That fact doesn't
detract from the act* is another disturbing sequence. A man innocently named Redding creates tiny havoc: *Redding, reading from
his prepared text.* Such unlucky combinations, which are easily
remedied, create a buzzing in the reader's head that distracts from
the business at hand.

Simplicity Will Do

Tone, as we have seen, varies widely, depending on the story,
the subject, the skill of writers, the passions of copy desks, and the
preferences of editors. Tone is not the same at *The Wall Street
Journal, The New York Times,* the *New York Post* and the *Los
Angeles Times.*

By and large, though, the most effective journalistic tone in the
'90s would seem to be the plain and unadorned. That at least is the
premise of this book. It is a tone that speaks to readers, not at
them, that explains, but doesn't lecture—conversational, perhaps,
but correct, never shrill and jazzed up.

Here's an example of the plain tone, taken from a story by AP
Special Correspondent Jules Loh about the shooting of the town
bully, the sort of story that often lures writers with a less disciplined ear into a rat-tat-tat, melodramatic style:

> He wasn't a street brawler. He was specific. He struck fear in your
> soul by staring you down, flashing a gun, occasionally using it. If you
> were his prey for today he stalked you. He glared at you in silence and
> when he spoke it was in a slow whisper. Chilling.
>
> He was born on a farm just outside of town. When he was a boy he fell
> off a hay wagon, requiring a steel plate to be implanted in his head.
> Some wondered if that was what made him so mean.
>
> This is a small town: 440 people, filling station, bank, post office, tav-
> ern, blacktop street, grain elevator. Beyond lie rolling meadows, rip-
> ening corn, redwing blackbirds, fat cattle, windmills and silos, a scene
> off a Sweet Lassy feed calendar.
>
> Ken McElroy jarred that pastoral serenity. So it is with outspoken
> relief that the citizens of Nodaway County now speak of him in the
> past tense. He is dead. The fear he brought them, though, still lingers
> in a new, unexpected form. . . .

Whatever gradations of tone you adopt, there can be no doubt about its importance for the writer. Barbara Tuchman, the historian, whose vivid prose combined with scholarship made her books best-sellers, said in an essay on her craft: "One learns to write by the practice thereof. After seven years' apprenticeship in journalism I have discovered that an essential element for good writing is a good ear. One must listen to the sound of one's own prose. This, I think, is one of the failures of much American writing. Too many writers do not listen to the sound of their own prose."

So listen.

PITFALLS: Attributive Verbs and Loaded Words
7

Among attributive verbs, *said* usually says it best. It's short, clear, neutral and unfailingly accurate, a verb for all seasons.

You'll need substitutes occasionally to avoid monotony, but be careful; they are not true synonyms of *said*, not even—especially not—*stated* or *declared*.

Each attributive verb carries its own shade of meaning and must fit your context, a requirement remarkably often overlooked. *"Shut up," he explained*, is a fiction writer tongue in cheek. *"The sun rises every day," she recalled*, is a news writer foot in mouth.

Attributives kindle a craving for elegance in misguided souls, who reach for archaisms like *averred* or *asseverated*. One newspaper rolled its own attributive, with shaky results: *"The costs were rather higher than we anticipated," she assessed.*

You can still find some editors and writers who consider the repetition of an attributive verb within a 500-word radius a disgrace: Seen in print was a chaste initial *said* followed by *asserted, averred, proclaimed, avowed, propounded* and *opined.*

The mounting suspense in following such a gaudy series was more gripping than the story. Let's consider the behavior of some widely used attributive verbs, listed in rough order of their usefulness:

went on	insisted	cautioned	predicted
continued	maintained	explained	
added	complained	recalled	

The words in the first column are plain and as neutral as *said*. The others are simply descriptive; just make sure they fit the circumstances.

The following can be hazardous:

pointed out	warned	claimed
noted	charged	

To say that a speaker *points out* something invests it with an aura of fact. The reader mentally supplies "the fact that" after the verb. This means that *point out* can have editorial nuances: *"The Democrats have seldom done this nation much good,"* the mayor *pointed out* seems to subscribe to the mayor's verdict. When there's no such risk, confine *pointed out* to instances when a speaker calls attention to something that might otherwise be overlooked: *"The police weren't legally required to use a warrant in this case,"* the attorney general pointed out.

Noted has similar connotations of fact and is even duller than *pointed out*.

Warned should be confined to quotes that point to genuine danger. Avoid lending credence to rhetorical overkill: *"A Republican victory will mean the end of civilization as we know it,"* the candidate warned.

Charged is best left to legal contexts: *"The company has willfully broken the public trust,"* the attorney general charged. Don't use the word when casual criticism or mild complaints are involved: *"Some employees are stretching their coffee breaks to unconscionable lengths,"* the director charged.

Claimed is a far remove from the neutral *said*. For reasons to be cautious, see the discussion of *claim* on page 77.

The following attributives are widely misused.

asserted	remarked	revealed
stated	commented	
declared	observed	

Asserted, stated, declared are often indiscriminately used for *said*. All are stronger and much more formal. To *assert* means to put forward an opinion or position strongly held. When that's done, the statement will speak for itself without benefit of that stiff *asserted*. *Stated* shouldn't be used at all; it is the instant mark of a wooden writer. (It fits if you're quoting from a deposition, but still looks dusty.) You *declare* a war, an emergency or martial law; the verb is too ponderous for most quotes.

Remarked applies to casual statements only: *"It's a fine day,"* he *remarked*. Not: *"Unless the Soviet Union withdraws from Afghanistan, our relations will continue on the present level,"* the spokesman *remarked*.

Commented also connotes the offhand, incidental, expressing a personal reaction or attitude: *"This is hardly his best work,"* the principal *commented*.

Observed is close in meaning to *remarked* and *commented*, but less conversational in tone and therefore less desirable.

God *reveals*, saints and mystics *reveal*; ordinary mortals *disclose*. Science may *reveal* a grand new cosmic concept, but a pediatrician *discloses* a new cure for colic.

All of the following keep cropping up in newsprint, which is regrettable:

avowed	exclaimed
averred	quipped
opined	snapped

Avowed involves a strong moral commitment and is almost always overly dramatic. Its cousin, *vowed*, suggests a solemn oath, possibly sealed with blood from an index finger. *Promised* and *pledged* are invariably better.

Averred and *opined* should be relegated to Gothic novels or specialists in musty prose. *Exclaimed* usually underscores something that doesn't need underscoring.

Quipped is pointless when a real quip is quoted; too often the writer applies it to a lame remark that lacks bite.

A person may possibly *snap* one word, but hardly a sentence.

This last attributive verb brings us to applied physiology. Never use verbs denoting non-verbal processes as attributives, like *smiled, wept, laughed, chortled, growled.* You don't smile words; you say them, smiling. *"I'm fond of him," she smiled,* is no better than *"I'm very hot this morning," he radiated.*

Beware Loaded Words

Some words can carry writers beyond what they intend to say and import value judgments into stories where they don't belong.

Reform is one such double-edged word. It means "to make better by removing faults or defects." That's why politicians, lawmakers, and advocates attach "reform" to programs they're pushing.

But one group's reform can be another group's calamity. Tax changes labeled *reform* might leave half the electorate fuming. *Abortion law reform* may be welcomed as such by one side and abhorred by the other.

So unless you're dealing with changes that the vast majority of reasonable citizens regard as beneficial, you had better steer clear of calling them a reform on your own. Call them changes or revisions. If *reform* appears in the title of a bill or program that annoys as many as it pleases, make clear that *reform* is what the sponsors call it, not you.

Here are some other words to watch:

Admit, as in admitting a crime, implies yielding reluctantly under pressure. *The company chairman admitted that interest rates had not been factored into production estimates* suggests that he came clean after an astute reporter put the thumbscrews to him. In fact, he volunteered the information. Use *said* or *acknowledged.*

Bureaucrat. A slighting term for *official, civil servant, government employee.*

Candidly, frankly. The defense attorney said frankly that his case rested on a single witness. How do you know he was frank? Why not let statements speak for themselves, without such comments?

Claim is not a synonym for *say, assert* or *argue.* You *claim* a (disputed) right. In a sentence like *the policeman claimed that he saw the gun* the verb casts doubt on his statement. The word is used precisely in this sentence: *The company lawyers claimed that the patents extended to fast-film paper as well.* There's doubt, to be resolved in court. For the same reason, *"I'm a better singer than most of the younger performers," the diva claimed,* is sensible usage. But *"I've been in the Metropolitan Opera for 23 years," she claimed,* is silly if the statement she made is factual.

Loophole. Like *scheme* or *scheming,* the noun connotes sly, devious, perhaps unethical proceedings. That's not the case when taxpayers take advantage of such breaks as the tax laws afford them. On the other hand, it's fair to write of a loophole when a lawyer discovers a way out of a contract due to an oversight that's plainly counter to the intent of the agreement.

Only. Even this worm can turn: *Only five of the nine administration measures got off the ground* suggests that the White House is fumbling.

Scheme. That's not another word for *plan,* just as *schemer* isn't the same as *planner.* A *scheme* suggests something shifty. That's not what the writer wanted to imply in, *American Airlines disclosed a scheme to lure new customers.*

Straightforward, steadfast. Characterizations that imply approval, just as *stubborn* implies disapproval. Some will consider the president's holding to his course as steadfast, others as stubborn.

QUOTES: Your Words or Mine?

8

News, to a remarkable degree, is what people say and how they say it—as actors in events, kibitzers, witnesses, informants, as movers and shakers, and as the moved and the shaken. The chatter is incessant. So are the news writer's efforts to distill useful quotes from it.

Quotes, as even novices quickly realize, are indispensable. They lend authenticity. They put readers in touch with people as directly as print can manage it. A story of any length that lacks quotes is as barren as a lunar landscape.

In his book, *The Craft of Interviewing*, Tom Brady extols quotes as "those brief, brilliant bursts of life." Ideally, that's what they are. Unfortunately, though, many quotes are neither brief nor brilliant but lifeless and verbose.

This isn't necessarily the news writer's fault. When people don't scintillate, you won't get scintillating quotes. But you can be selective about what you use. Too many writers seem to assume that quotation marks, by themselves, can transform a grunt into a great fugue. *Smith said he accepted the job because it represented a "challenge."* They help not at all.

In leisurely interviews and other setpieces, skilled reporters can patiently cast their lines until a few gaudy fish rise to the bait. In the hot pursuit of ordinary news, there's much less opportunity for that. Quotes are often snatched on the run: A hasty comment from a harassed lawyer, a cop's police blotter prose, the handful of dust stirred up by a bureaucrat scuttling for cover under a barrage of words.

All you can do with the stuff, by way of direct quotes, is to take it or leave it. Like other facts, quotes are not subject to revision. Once words are enclosed by quotation marks, they must be what the source said. Attempts to "improve" that by reshuffling or even changing words are high crimes and misdemeanors. The furthest you can go is to fix minor grammatical errors and omit pure padding or meaningless repetition.

When to Quote?

Under these constraints, the art of handling quotes comes down to knowing when to quote, when to paraphrase, when to forget the whole thing. Sometimes the choice is simple. When a Navy secretary responds to reproaches that he's not sufficiently committed by saying, *"Lemmings are great team players, and see where they wind up,"* you quote him. When a preacher, threatened by Texas officials with shutting down a home for wayward girls, says, *"It may be the ninth inning and we may be behind in the score, but I see my bases loaded and Jesus Christ coming to bat,"* you'd hit that pitch out of the ballpark.

Most quotes aren't nearly so picturesque. When they sink below a certain level a succinct paraphrase is the answer:

The senator said that "during this period of time, which covered six years, the subcommittee held a total of only six days of hearings."	The senator said the subcommittee held only six days of hearings in as many years.

The main distinction of the senatorial statement is 10 superfluous words.

Some matter shouldn't be quoted at all:

"I have presented to his excellency, President Hrawi, my letters of credence accrediting me as ambassador . . . of the United States to Lebanon," Crocker told reporters after the 30-minute ceremony

This is not electrifying. The following is sheer skullduggery:

This suggests, the study said, that "although parents may be able to affect their children's cognitive skill acquisition, they may have relatively little influence on the ultimate level attained."

Occasionally, less than incisive remarks are worth direct quotation for the insight they give. A New York legislator, when asked about corruption in the state Assembly:

"Personally speaking, for myself, to the best of my knowledge, I don't think I know anything, to the best of my knowledge."

Good quotes should summarize what's on a person's mind, crystallize an emotion or attitude, offer an individual perspective of some sort—preferably in a concise and interesting way.

Two examples, both from *The New York Times*. Here's a woman quoted in an account of life in Nicaragua:

"We can't make ends meet," said a 36-year-old waitress and mother of three who lives in the capital. "Everything's going up. We used to buy meat most days, but that's out of the question. We have to line up for hours for sugar and rice. And then we're told we can't have wage increases."

And this from a story about Northern Ireland's Maze prison, where IRA men were starving themselves to death:

"By the time they get in here, there's no more belligerence, no more fight," said an attendant in the one-story, 10-bed hospital. "They're really quite cooperative and polite at this final stage. They just sit there and quietly die."

A paraphrase would have been sinful.

What is said doesn't have to be remarkable in itself to carry a story forward. But note the difference the direct quotes make in this amusing intro:

Yesterday was just one of those days for Jose Cruz. He got lectured by an 84-year-old grandmother, was surrounded by cops and arrested on two felonies after a seven-hour standoff.

"I'm sorry, Ruth," said Cruz, 29, as police led him in handcuffs from the apartment of Ruth Wolko, whom he had held hostage in her fifth-floor apartment in Riverdale, Bronx.

Earlier, Wolko told friends she had fed her captor a nice kosher breakfast and asked him, "Is this the only profession you have?"

When he answered, "Yes," she said, "Maybe you should go into some other profession."

It began about 5 a.m. when Cruz allegedly was discovered looting a fourth-floor apartment.

When quotation marks, with their small subliminal drumroll, signal a human voice, the reader expects a pitch different from dryly factual recitation. Nothing but disappointment in the following story:

MIAMI—More than 6,300 exotic birds, from tiny finches to large parrots and macaws worth as much as $5,000 apiece, have been destroyed at an import center because of an outbreak of Newcastle disease, a virus that kills domestic poultry, federal officials said.

"All the birds here were destroyed and we are in the process of cleaning and disinfecting the area," said Connie Crunkelton, a spokeswoman for the U.S. Department of Agriculture.

Miss Crunkelton said federal officials feared that infected birds may have been shipped from Pet Farms Inc., the import company, within the past 30 days.

"We have notified the animal health officials in the states known to have received shipments," she said. "They will go to the facility and see if there are any infected birds. If so, they will have to be destroyed and the owners will be reimbursed for their loss."

There were 123 species and subspecies among the 6,300 birds destroyed at Pet Farms, Miss Crunkelton said. The owner will be reimbursed for the loss, she said.

"We don't have a dollar estimate on the birds as of yet, but we expect one later," Miss Crunkelton said.

Putting such pedestrian, fact-sheet information into direct quotation is like trying to set the telephone directory to music. A few words of paraphrase could have dispatched the details.

The Uses of Quotes

Besides adding living voices to the script, quotes perform certain standard functions. They are used to:

- Document and support third-person statements in the lead and elsewhere.
- Set off controversial material, where the precise wording can be an issue, as in legal contexts.

- Catch distinctions and nuances in important passages of speeches and convey some of the flavor of the speaker's language.
- Highlight exchanges and testimony in trials, hearings, meetings and other garrulous encounters.

Quotes should pull lustily on the oars to help move the story along, as in this example:

> SAN SALVADOR (AP)—Terrorists fired three anti-tank rocket grenades at the United States Embassy today, causing some damage but apparently no injuries, security forces reported.
>
> They said the grenades were probably fired from a building about 60 yards away from the embassy compound.
>
> "Something put a hole in one of our upper stories, but as far as we can tell nobody was hurt," said an embassy spokesman reached by telephone.
>
> Another embassy employee said the damage was on the third floor, which houses the office of Ambassador Robert E. White, but the ambassador was not in the embassy at the time.

The third graf backs up the lead and adds a bit of fresh detail. Repetition is the great danger. Even robust quotes turn sickly as a reprise of something that's just been reported in third-person:

> The chairman announced that the company would start the most ambitious engineering project in its history.
>
> "We'll launch our most ambitious engineering project ever," he told applauding stockholders.

Pertinence May Decide

Newsworthy speeches, whether scintillating or not, require considerable direct quotation. Since you're usually working from a text you can browse for quotes at some leisure. Here pertinence overrides color: It's advisable to give significant passages in the speaker's own words even if they are fairly tedious.

This was not a problem in the following example, a happy meeting between a strong expressive text and a writer, John Edlin, who knew how to make the most of it from cutting the partial quote of the lead to the extended quotation in the last paragraph:

SALISBURY, Zimbabwe (AP)—Prime Minister Robert Mugabe said Thursday the black states of southern Africa must free themselves from foreign economic exploitation that has made them either "puppets or perpetual beggars."

Mugabe, opening the ministerial session of the Southern African Development Coordination Conference at a Salisbury hotel, accused unscrupulous foreign investors of maintaining a relentless grip on southern Africa's resources.

"We remain dominated economically by economic lords as we were politically dominated by political lords yesterday," said the prime minister of newly independent Zimbabwe, the former British colony of Rhodesia. "Economic domination is indeed a worse phenomenon than political domination."

Mugabe said, "Our resources are wasting away day by day as they get freighted to Paris, London and New York."

He said the nine nations taking part in the conference on "economic liberation" have recognized that they are "fragmented, grossly exploited, and subject to economic manipulation by outsiders."

The prime minister particularly criticized multinational corporations which he said arrange a "mouse's share for us and a lion's share for themselves." Black African nations, he said, are imprisoned by unfavorable trading conditions. They sell their raw material cheaply but have to pay "exorbitant" prices for imports.

"Thus we meet foul play in both cases," he said. "And whether we play at home or away, ours is perpetual defeat, theirs perpetual victory. Is it any wonder that we have been turned into either economic puppets or perpetual beggars?"

The reader has enough in Mugabe's own words to judge both substance and tone of his argument and catch a glint of his personality as well.

Help Wanted (Sometimes)

Quotes sometimes need a little internal stitching. A parenthetic insert may be used to explain a technical word or to clarify a pronoun reference: *"He said he had no idea why he (Smith) didn't show up for work with the others."* But a little stage-whispering goes a long way. It's drowning out the quote here:

"I guess he (the driver) just hates hitchhikers. They (highway motorists) do it all the time. They swerve at you like they're trying to hit you. This is the first time one of us (referring to highway tramps in general) ever really got hit."

When a quote needs that much help, you're better off paraphrasing.

The ellipsis (. . .) indicates omitted matter. The trouble is that it calls attention to what is not rather than to what is. It's sometimes necessary, for example in quoting government reports or legal documents, when sentences are excerpted from a coherent larger passage. But an ellipsis is seldom required in the ordinary run of conversational and interview quotes, which readers know to be excerpts anyway.

Clues and identification enabling readers to understand a quote normally should precede rather than follow it; the cryptic quote at the start of a paragraph is an annoyance.

> That optimism assumed that passengers would return fairly quickly, airline executives say. But doubts about safety, along with a soft economy, have kept large numbers of passengers away, producing grim near-term prospects for several carriers.
>
> "I don't agree with that," said an airline official about the view that the carriers would profit from the slowdown.

The reader is momentarily misled into believing that the disagreement refers to the grim near-term prospects.

The *Said of* Trap

Writers sometimes plunge into the *said of* mode to clarify something that's already clear from the context:

> While the players did not know that Michael was on the verge of being dismissed yesterday, they knew his job had been on the line at least once this season and, based on their experience, they knew that the team's principal owner often pressures and embarrasses his employees in a belief that it will improve their performance.
>
> "That may work in one facet of life but not in this one," Watson *said of* Steinbrenner's techniques.
>
> "Stick will be here," George Steinbrenner *said of* him that day last November.

Another example:

"It's rare. We don't usually get that many large petitions," Richard Markse, a railroad spokesman, *said of* the 300 signatures Fields collected.

More clearly put:

Fields collected 300 signatures. "It's rare," said Richard Markse, a railroad spokesman. "We don't usually get that many large petitions."

From a story about a dowser's trade:

"I feel a little tingle and it starts moving," Austin *said of* his divining rod.

Clueing the reader in more effectively:

Describing the workings of his divining rod, Austin said, "I feel a little tingle and it starts moving."

Haphazard Attribution

Make sure the reader always knows who's speaking, but don't overattribute in running quotations:

"I call that dead water. I can't find dead water in underground caverns." Austin calls moving water "love water" and says that is the only water he can find. "It's got to have some movement to it," *the dowser said*.

Don't drop attribution haphazardly into a quote where it will disrupt the flow of a sentence:

"The charge is not," the lawyer said, "warranted in the slightest degree."

"This is the second time," the angry senator said, "the agency has violated its own regulations."

Put the sinuous lawyer and the angry senator at the start or at the end of their sentences. When attribution goes within a sentence, it should fit smoothly between clauses or where a speaker might naturally pause:

"I thought I'd be free long before then," she said, "but it hasn't worked out that way."

Fragmentary Quotes

An indiscriminate rage to quote, or perhaps a sense of insecurity, traps writers into pointless fragmentary quotes, consisting of one or two unremarkable words used in their ordinary sense:

> The mayor said a "key" element of his plan was the parking complex. He noted it had the support of "many citizens."

> The critic called it a "wonderful" movie.

Had our critic called it "incandescent," however, quotation marks would be proper. The word is sufficiently unusual to rate the epaulets.

The quotation marks also are justified in cases like the following:

> When arrested, Smith said he was an "importer." (*To convey doubt.*)

> The president said Reagan was in no sense a "racist." (*To make clear that the president himself used this highly charged word.*)

> The Soviet news agency Tass said today that "criminal activities" had occurred in Kabul. (*In the West, it was called something else.*)

Watch the Context

Next to getting the actual words right, the most important thing is to keep quotes in context. Failure usually arises from careless compression that makes a statement appear more emphatic than it is. A qualification may be dropped or buried, a speaker's elaboration of a point overlooked, or a remark intended as jocular reported deadpan.

It may be tiresome when a newsmaker surrounds his assertions with *ifs, buts* and *maybes,* but if he elects to crawl, the writer must not force him into a trot.

Special caution is indicated with the use of partial quotes in leads. Qualifications should either stay within the quote or follow immediately. Even if the full quote, with its amplified or softened meaning, appears later in the story, it's not enough; the reader may not get that far.

Consider the full statement on the left and the new version on the right:

| "There may be occasions, crimes, when the death penalty appears justified. At least many people think so. I have sometimes leaned that way myself, but to my mind, large problems always remain." | A longtime opponent of capital punishment said today that on occasions "the death penalty appears justified."
"I have sometimes leaned that way myself," he added, though "large problems always remain." |

The partial quotes are accurate, but the meaning—the tentative tone—has been subtly altered.

Not so subtle is what befell James Watt, secretary of the interior under Reagan, who found himself sandbagged with a striking sentence that was widely quoted without the rest of the passage.

At a congressional hearing, Watt was asked if he believed that some resources should be conserved for future generations. His full reply:

"Absolutely. That is the delicate balance the secretary of the interior must have to be steward for the natural resources for this generation as well as future generations. *I do not know how many future generations we can count on before the Lord returns.* Whatever it is, we have to manage with a skill to have the resources for future generations."

Perhaps an official sophisticated about the ways of the media should have scented peril in injecting religious musings into his testimony, but those who seized on the italicized sentence in isolation certainly conveyed a meaning different from that of the complete passage. It's something the conscientious news writer will guard against.

You can also skewer a quote by converting a long, involved question into the subject's answer:

Reporter: *Do you feel the verdict was wrong, that it was a gross miscarriage of justice?*

A: *Well, yes.*

Copy: *He said he "felt that the verdict was wrong and a gross miscarriage of justice."*

Did he? Reporters shouldn't ask speechifying questions, but some will, especially at televised news conferences. You deal with it by clearly differentiating: *He said "yes" to a reporter's question whether he felt, etc.*

In the following passage, the practice is carried to absurdity:

> Eighty-seven percent of those surveyed in the national poll said they "feel personally, deeply involved with the fate of the hostages and are willing to wait as long as necessary to get the hostages back unharmed."

Must have been an interesting chorus. The quote, of course, refers to the survey question.

Never attribute a direct quote to more than one person, unless you've stumbled on a tribe that speaks in unison. The following appeared in a newspaper:

> Feminists hurled abuse as the men competed in a Bavarian park to become the fastest tree planter. "We don't accept the perpetuation of the masculine image," they yelled.

The *New Yorker* ran the item under the heading, "Yells We Doubt Ever Got Yelled."

Overextended Attribution

Although indirect quotation offers more latitude, there are similar traps. Be sure not to attribute to the source wording and coloring obviously different from the source's own:

> WASHINGTON—The nation's unemployment rate shot up from 6.2 percent to 7 percent in April, the highest level in 2½ years *and a powerful sign that the inflation-wracked economy is now being squeezed by the rise of recession,* the government reported today.

All very true, no doubt, but that's not how the government's report put it.

In the following instance, the attribution is just overextended:

> "It affects your whole life," said Wilson's pretty wife, Nancy, whose job as a court clerk helps to sustain them. "You're on edge. It's like a disease you're waiting to catch."
>
> The disease has reached epidemic proportions in the black community, which suffers from a jobless rate of 30 percent, says the Rev. Thomas Robinson, head of the Opportunity Industrialization Center.

The Rev. Mr. Robinson, however, didn't say anything about diseases and epidemics. A period after *community* and a new sentence would keep things straight.

A Band-Aid May Help

We have stressed that direct quotes must faithfully reproduce what the speaker has said. There are times, however, when in an interview, minor grammatical slips could be corrected; hardly anyone is free of such mistakes in casual speech. The purpose is not to make anyone look good, but to make things easier for the reader.

For example, a story quoted Secretary of the Treasury Regan as saying: "Jim Baker knows more about politics than I'll ever know. But I think I know more about finances than *him.*" The writer could safely have made that *he,* or, better yet, stopped the quote at *finances.*

Note we are talking about mini-adjustments. Heroic intervention to straighten out gaping incoherencies is another matter. When a politican, say, replies to a question in a way that betrays monumental trouble in coming to grips with it, don't tighten and smooth quotes into a masterpiece of concise statement. Judgment, fairness and evenhandedness are the guides to navigating these shoals.

What about people who speak generally poor English, street language, use *ain't* and *that there's?* How far you go in using offbeat idiom depends on the purpose of the story. If it's to portray life in the Appalachian hollows, snippets of non-standard English, peculiar phrasing, the occasional double negative will add depth and flavor without offense.

But in most news stories, such speechways are simply irrelevant. You might call attention to a man's limp if he's just entered a track meet, but not if he's walking to the subway.

To illustrate from a story about a tavern shooting in Oregon:

No motive for the shooting was established.

"He didn't say nothing," said Brent Yagle, a patron of the popular nightspot frequented by people mostly in their 20s. "He just opened the door and started firing. I didn't think the shots were real until I saw people drop."

The tavern owner, John Helton, said, "I do hope he had some kind of reason and didn't do it just 'cause he was in the mood."

The double negative and bobtailed *because* merely contribute a whiff of condescension. Better to paraphrase the first: *The man said nothing, according to Brent Yagle* . . . And spelling out *because* would have violated no higher truth.

The following underscores the distinctions involved in this minor housebreaking. Saul Pett plumbed the mood of Asheville, N.C., in an election year. His intro centers on a series of quotes:

> "Half this country keeps the other half going," says a bitter housewife in line at the checkout counter. Ahead of her is a man buying more meat than she can afford. He pays with food stamps.
>
> "We can't do anything about those crazy Iranians holding our people," writes a rural editorialist, "but we can do something about taxes. We can control them."
>
> "I'm relatively affluent, but will I be able to send my kids to college?" asks the executive director of what used to be a pillar of American optimism, the local Chamber of Commerce.
>
> "The election?" ponders an old mountaineer. "I *ain't* heard it mentioned except on the TV."

The last quotee appears in the character of a mountaineer, an archetype, you might say, and the *ain't* is as natural as the plug of tobacco in a pitcher's cheek. No need to paraphrase.

Expletive Deleted

Profanity, vulgarity and obscenity present another kind of problem. Society has become vastly more permissive toward them in most forms of print, films and theaters. Newspapers, however, still avoid using such expressions—on grounds of taste in dealing with a very diversified audience, and also because blue language in a medium of information mostly distracts readers from the business at hand.

The limits of the acceptable vary from newspaper to newspaper. Each has its own well-defined policy (which doesn't preclude occasional soul-searching).

It's good advice—and AP policy—to avoid casual profanity and vulgarisms. Many swear words and expletives are so routine at certain levels of conversation in many groups that they're like other verbal fillers that can simply be dropped from a direct quote. When that seems awkward, paraphrase.

The practical test on admitting expletives is whether they are essential to the story. They seldom are. A celebrated exception was Jimmy Carter's unpresidential language referring to Sen. Edward Kennedy in promising to "*whip his ass.*" Even so, some papers fig-leafed the noun with dashes or asterisks.

Since Carter's day, reticence toward "ass-kicking" in high places has diminished. George Bush has been quoted to that effect at least twice, as vice president and president.

The mild profanity in the following example is also indispensable in giving the earthy flavor of a tough lady who had kept federal inspectors off her coal mine at gunpoint:

> When her cousin tried to fetch her she leveled a pistol at him and told him to get lost. A masher got fresh once while she was waiting tables and she scalded him with coffee. Her refusal of favors to another man included smashing his windshield with a tire iron. Don't cross Violet Smith.
>
> "Hell, kid, them feds have never scared me.
>
> "One time when I was running a little grocery in Durango, an Internal Revenue agent came in and said I haven't paid my taxes. I had. I flattened the S.O.B. with my fist and kicked his rear end out of the door."
>
> Violet Smith, incidentally, does not abbreviate S.O.B.

Paraphrase to the Rescue

A few final points on quotes:

• We're not in the business of protecting people from their own flapping tongues, but it's poor practice to make somebody look foolish in print when he has innocently misspoken himself:

> "What is lacking is not indifference and apathy," suggests Joseph Guinn, vice president of the association. "The general public just doesn't understand the educational value."

He meant that apathy and indifference were not the problem, and both he and the reader should have been rescued by paraphrase.

• Here you have the right way and the wrong way of using fragmentary quotes in one sentence:

ATLANTA—A police officer testified today that he stopped Wayne B. Williams near a Chattahoochee River bridge because a "loud splash" made the officer "pretty suspicious."

The first phrase doesn't rate the quotation marks; the second does, as the precise description of his feelings.

• The more quotes resemble dialogue in form, the livelier they are. An exchange gives readers a special sense of participation. Here's an example from a routine news conference:

Dick Moe, an aide to the vice president, told reporters: "I think both sides are in a position to go to the other and, depending on who prevails, seek their support in the general election."
"And get it?" he was asked.
"And get it."

In some stories, usually features, it's possible to trim super-structure for a similarly crisp effect. Compare the elaborate setups on the left with the version on the right:

When asked if she admired her mother's cooking, Miss Johnson replied, "It was fabulous."	What of her mother's cooking? "Fabulous." Her own? "Not so hot."
In response to a query about her own cooking skill, she conceded it was "not so hot."	

• Partial quotes should fit into the grammatical structure of the sentence.

The chairman emphasized that he "insists on equal pay for equal work."

Did he say, *"I insists?"* No. So move the opening quotation mark or paraphrase.

• Avoid double attribution:

The commissioner said he would move promptly against what he called "an outrageous situation."

Either *what he called* or the quotation marks, but not both.

• As in a primitive ritual, certain quotes recur automatically in similar news situations. People have many times read or heard those phrases and will mouth them when opportunity offers. By now these quotes have the appeal of bovine cud. But unless someone breaks the chain, they will continue until they become the last syllables of recorded time. Here are a few such prefabricated phrases that ought to be passed by:

"It's a great challenge." Starlet about her new role, executive about his new job, coach on taking over a team of ragged bums.

"I like people," in various nauseating configurations. Worth quoting if a mass murderer says it.

"It sounded like 10 (15, 100) freight trains." Applicable to all tornadoes.

"It sounded like an atom bomb going off." Any explosion. If he's actually heard an atom bomb going off, write about him.

COLOR:
Dip Your Brush
in Small Details

9

Elsewhere in this book we discuss how reporters need to develop a good ear to fit words together gracefully. To fit words together colorfully, they need to develop a good eye.

For color implies a way of *seeing* a story so you can *show* the reader. Adjectives and intensifiers have nothing to do with it— they are, in fact, great deceivers.

Why inform readers that something is dramatic or tragic? Give them the particulars, and they will supply their own adjectives.

What real image do you call up by describing a resort as *posh* or a military reservation as *sprawling*? What's distinctive about the *white, sandy* beach? Most beaches are. Or about the city that *is a city of many contrasts*? The same can be written about every city, and probably has been.

Color is a matter of the right details—observed directly, elicited from witnesses, always with the breath of actuality. It works even in a report as routine as one on a city council hearing:

As the hearing droned on past midnight, half the audience had left. But the woman in the front row was still knitting away at her red sweater. In back, a middle-aged man, head down, was snoring gently. Councilman Smithers seemed to be counting the patches of peeling plaster on the walls, while Saunders rested his chin on the gavel. There was no further need of pounding.

Tiny details and a splash of real color in an unlikely setting. How many reporters would have gone to the trouble?

Here's a passage from a column by the late Red Smith, describing a morning at the race track:

> Through the fragrance of the wood fires burning under the elms in the stable area behind Saratoga's main track, wreaths of morning mist curled up to be burned away by slanting rays of sunshine. Hot-walkers led horses in lazy circles behind the barns, while other horses stood relishing the flow of cold water from garden hoses trained on their forelegs.
>
> Grooms swathed horses with soapy sponges and rubbed them dry. The rhythmic throbbing of hooves could be heard from the track itself, where the horses were working.

And here's an AP story, in an entirely different vein. Again, the scene is set with strong particulars:

> Like a candy bar in the hands of a 2-year-old, crude oil from the Exxon Valdez has gotten into everything.
>
> Globs of mousse litter the cobbled beach. Rainwater beads up on rocks as on the waxed hood of a car. A cleanup worker digs into the sand and his hand comes up a greasy brown.
>
> A burly fisherman breaks into tears as he describes steering his boat through the slick: no water lapping, no birds crying, just the sickening silence of oil slipping past the hull.
>
> At a bird rescue center in Seward, some of the patients are failing. They have been washed clean, but not before swallowing fatal doses of oil. They don't cry out; instinct tells them not to advertise their distress to predators. "They just get real quiet, sit in a corner and die," says rescue coordinator Jay Holcomb.

Small, Specific Detail

For color, reporters cannot rely on phrases and fancy—or ready-made—figures of speech. They rely on hard particulars. They must train themselves to spot those small, specific details that give intimate glimpses into the nature of the subject.

Jules Loh, in a profile of Herbert Hoover, noticed that among many items on the former president's desk was a tumbler containing a dozen well-sharpened pencils—a detail that most good reporters would pick up. But he also noticed that the erasers on the pencils were worn down. That detail told more about the man the pencils were worn down. That detail told more about the man than all the obvious ones: the color of his necktie, the shine on his shoes, the handkerchief in his breast pocket.

When Pulitzer Prize laureate Saul Pett wrote a story on the workings of the mind of Robert McNamara, he never once used the words *mind like a computer*. He didn't have to. He conveyed this idea by attention to detail during a dinner interview, describing McNamara as:

> . . . judiciously weighing the options of having a second drink or not, evaluating all the factors in selecting between fish or beef and, once having made up his mind, never looking back.

Sometimes it's difficult or inconvenient to plod after details, but that's where Joe Smith, the writer, relies on Joe Smith, the reporter. AP Newsfeatures writer Sid Moody discussed this in a postscript to a story he wrote about an ocean crossing on a square-rigged Norwegian sailing ship:

> You're looking for detail, verbs of description instead of adjectives or adverbs. Sure, the helmsman stands at the wheel like a Viking. But he also clamps his lips into a line to keep out the rain, narrows his eyes to gunslits against the wind, stares transfixed as a swami at the compass light. His knuckles are white from the cold and the strain of the helm. He sails on. The reader may have his own idea of what a Viking is, but you're out there in the wet to tell him what this particular Viking did on this particular ship in this particular storm, and if you can't give him specifics, you might as well go below and be warm and dry and eat goat yogurt.

Pseudo-Color Won't Work

No, grand generalizations and indistinct noun-adjective combinations don't add color to writing; particulars do. Here's an example of pseudo-color from a news story about a newly appointed immigration commissioner:

> Outside the state capitol he is said to be essentially mild-mannered. With his modishly styled hair, neat mustache and hornrimmed glasses, he could be taken for a professor from the nearby University of Texas.

On the basis of that description, so could half the male population. And note the ponderous qualifier before that daring characterization, mild-mannered. Pope John Paul II is mild-mannered, and so was Willie Sutton, the bank robber. Finally, what does a college professor look like? There are college professors who could be taken for plumbers, undertakers, corporation chairmen, engineers and confidence men.

This kind of mush just amounts to a string of words, adding up to a cliché portrayal that you've read before in a thousand inconsequential contexts.

Contrast this terse sentence in an AP story describing a craftsman who reproduces Shaker furniture:

> Charles Caffal is a 43-year-old artisan, built along the lines he admires most. He is as lean as a clothespin—a Shaker invention—and his only ornamentation is a full, reddish beard.

This is a rich image in a few words, and a long way from the essentially mild-mannered, bespectacled gent who could be taken for your typical college professor.

So is this line:

> On hills that are normally green at this time, there's nothing but a sere, parched, dun-colored stubble.

Many writers have made a perfunctory bow to color with "drought-stricken hills." The quoted sentence is intensely visual. And that *sere*? A difficult word, no doubt, for many readers, but the sense of the passage is not impaired for the ignorant, while the knowing might take pleasure in the echo from Shakespeare's "sere and yellow leaf."

Not every story is suitable to color. A presidential announcement, a report on rising interest rates, various government actions—not much chance for visual writing there.

In fact, details squirted on austere facades where they don't belong merely irritate, like graffiti.

A story on the appearance of retired Chief Justice Warren Burger at a Senate hearing reports his sober testimony for 10 grafs. The 11th starts out, "The silver-haired Burger . . . " Not even his barber would care.

Somewhere in almost every story on Adm. Poindexter testifying at the Iran-Contra hearings, the adjective "pipe-puffing" surfaced, without ever achieving relevance.

A story on a woman desperately telephoning police for help notes—in the lead, no less—that her phone was "cream-colored." What's the difference?

In stories on court procedures, writers seem to feel compelled to describe the principals' clothes. That's OK if the prosecutor wears a leotard, but:

> Miller, wearing a tan suit over his large frame, took notes while Schiff delivered his opening statement. Miller's two sons, wearing gray business suits, were among the spectators.
>
> List, wearing a light-brown suit and tie, sat stone-faced . . .
>
> As Moore, wearing a long-sleeved shirt and tie, walked to the prison building . . .

Don't Overdo It

Flatness is a greater problem in news writing than excessive color, but color can be overdone.

A scuffle between two drunks, however picturesque, at a political gathering doesn't rate a burst of description high in a report of a presidential candidate's campaign speech. Like so much else in this intricate business, color requires a sense of balance and proportion, impossible to define, and every colorful detail must pass the test of relevance.

When you're trying too hard, this is what can happen:

> HOUSTON—Leaders of the seven richest nations convened today for a summit that could reshape the world's economic landscape to nourish the dizzying blossom of East-West peace and stem a tenacious underbrush of trade and environmental disputes among themselves.

The writer, having trained his eye to spot particulars with the intensity of a devout bird-watcher, must come to the typewriter with a notebook crammed with them. And then have the discipline to use only those details that tell something about the subject. Details painstakingly collected are not easy to discard. The writer is often tempted to use them because he has them. Which may be why, in countless celebrity interviews, we're told that

Miss Sexuality dispensed her bon mots over a tomato and water-cress salad. (Mention the menu if it's filleted rattlesnake.)

When Color Works

Let us conclude the dissertation on color with two examples where, integral to each story, color works exactly right.

The first is from a story that dealt with a controversy about convict road crews. After outlining the issues and describing the work, writer Andrew Petkofsky of the *Richmond News Leader* took his readers to the scene:

> The crew had started at the Henrico County line about a month before and worked steadily through some of the summer's hottest days.
>
> This day was cool and lovely, however, and the prisoners in blue work clothes and orange hard hats had plenty of time to gripe to a reporter as they hefted shovels, rakes and brooms. The uniformed young man standing guard with a 12-gauge shotgun listened impassively. He had heard it all before.

Note the precision of visual detail.

Second, consider this brushwork of vivid detail in a story by James A. Bacon in the *Roanoke* (Va.) *Times & World News*, about a millionaire down on his luck:

> Millions of dollars in debt, abandoned by friends and kin, Elkins was planning his comeback. A kitchen table, littered with dirty dishes and pizza crust, was his desk. An antiquated telephone dialed by the motel switchboard operator was his link to the outside world.
>
> Five years earlier, "Covey" Elkins had been the most dazzling success story in the Virginia coal fields. . . .
>
> Now the remnants of his empire are locked up in bankruptcy court. Gone is the mansion with its four-car garage, sauna and indoor swimming pool. Gone are the Lincoln Continentals, the helicopter, the fine clothes. And gone are the false friends and flatterers.
>
> On an ice-bound winter afternoon, Elkins worked in the gloom of his motel room, tying up the phone for hours, trying to drum up credit, old coal equipment, overlooked coal leases—anything that could put him back in business.

Color is a way of seeing a story. On behalf of reporters who prefer to operate on sonar, like bats, we can only intone the Old Testament verse: "Lord, I pray thee open his eyes that he may see."

PSEUDO-COLOR: Clichés and Other Trespasses

10

We now pass from living color into the nether world of clichés, misshapen figures of speech and strained comparisons. These, too, spring from the laudable impulse to brighten copy, but the tools are shoddy and so are the results.

Clichés by definition are threadbare phrases that good writers try to avoid. George Orwell, a purist in style, advised long ago: "Never use a metaphor, a simile, or a figure of speech that you are used to seeing in print."

The general idea is sound, but the prohibition too sweeping. No writer can do entirely without the large stock of familiar expressions that includes hardworking idiom, phrases somewhere between idiom and cliché (off base, snowed under) and clichés unalloyed.

The late Eric Partridge, who heroically compiled a *Dictionary of Clichés*, conceded that what constitutes a cliché is partly a matter of opinion. Set a brace of editors to hunting down clichés in the same story and some of their trophies will be different; one may gag at a phrase that doesn't ruffle the other.

The way in which you use a tired expression also bears on its cliché status. Sir Ernest Gowers, another accomplished word man, says it depends on whether clichés "are used unthinkingly as reach-me-downs or chosen as the best means of saying what a writer has to say."

Furthermore, not all clichés are obnoxious to the same degree. Some are so abysmal that no self-respecting writer will touch them in any context: *Selling like hotcakes, breath of fresh air, last but not least, shun like the plague, leave no stone unturned* are among the pariahs. (A selected list of other mangy expressions appears at the end of this chapter.)

But in many cases, no summary beheading is necessary. *Sour grapes, swing of the pendulum,* and *white elephant,* for example, are greatly worn. Yet each wraps up a rather complicated situation succinctly, and if your alternative proves labored and verbose, you're better advised to stick to the cliché.

Clichés at Arm's Length

Here are a few suggestions on dealing with clichés—at proper arm's length (cliché? idiom?) but without hysteria:

1. Don't worry about an occasional cliché, but start stringing a few together and your story wilts. With each additional cliché in a passage, the staleness increases exponentially. That's what happened in the following political story:

   1st graf: They're *throwing out the rule book* in Nassau County.

   3rd graf: Caso is *not taking it lying down.*

   7th graf: Some say Margiotta has not enforced the peace because (1) he is *licking elective wounds,* (2) he is *gun-shy* from federal investigations of several Republicans and wants to *shed his boss image* for a *low profile,* or (3) he believes it's the right thing to do.

   10th graf: In the spring, he announced his availability, widely regarded as a move to force Caso's maneuvers *out of the closet.*

No story can weather that many banalities. The last figure, incidentally, is not only a cliché, but a mangled one: politicians might maneuver in a smoke-filled room, but hardly in a closet.

Nor can a lead take off with this many bromides (and mixed metaphors besides):

> The stakes have never been higher as Secretary of State James A. Baker III returns to the U.N. stage with what appears to be a winning hand in a dangerous game of chicken with Iraqi President Saddam Hussein.

2. A cliché is acceptable when it serves your meaning precisely: *The city for years has tried to rid itself of these white elephants.* Never use a cliché as decoration or for emphasis; it has lost all power and glitter: *The rumor swept the town like wildfire.*

3. Don't use a cliché as a facetious way to inflate a simple idea: *By the end of the year, the long arm of the law had caught up with him.* (*The law had caught up with him.*)

4. When you must use a cliché, get it right. Don't *throw out the baby with the dishwater (bathwater).* Don't say, as a senator recently did, that *we're all working like banshees.* (Banshees *wail.*) Or make it, as a government secretary commenting on her boss's absence did, *when the wolf is away, the mice will play.* (Although that might have been a Freudian slip.)

5. It's impossible to freshen a cliché, so let it slide past quietly without tinkering with it. *They put the fancy cart before the old horse* merely underscores the poverty of the phrase.

6. Don't put clichés in quotation marks or apologize for them coyly with an *as the old cliché has it.* Inviting the reader to hold his nose just calls attention to the odor.

7. Don't dress up your copy with Great Quotations that have been ground into commonplaces: *East is East and West is West and never the twain shall meet* (Kipling); *a rose by any other name . . . the slings and arrows . . . to be or not to be,* (Shakespeare); *A rose is a rose is a rose,* (Gertrude Stein). I hope to see one income tax deadline pass without a story reminding us that April is the *cruelest month* (T. S. Eliot).

These and a hundred more, splendid in their original setting, have become debased currency by overborrowing.

8. If there is one way to squeeze juice from a cliché, it's by twisting it to yield a new and surprising meaning: *Bedfellows make strange politics.*

Sports Page Pariahs

Nowhere do clichés flourish more luxuriantly than on sports pages. It doesn't have to be this way, as good sportswriters prove every day. But the weaklings succumb in droves to the handy platitude.

There was a time when track teams were known, among other horrors, as thinclads, swimmers as tankmen, tennis players as netmen, baseballs as horsehides and footballs as pigskins. If these have mercifully died out, they have plenty of replacements.

There may be no excuse for such littering, but there's an explanation.

The subject matter, for one thing, is pretty much the same. Stanley Walker, one of the great newspapermen of any year, summed up one part of the problem nearly 50 years ago in his book *City Editor*: "Almost every murder, suicide, shipwreck and train collision is cut on a different pattern, and the reporter does not have to seek outlandish substitutes for common terms. One baseball game, however, is pretty much the same as any other. The few standard verbs and nouns used in writing of baseball, football and boxing become tiresome."

In short, as the event loses flavor, some reporters tend to over-season their prose; plain words like *defeat, win, score,* seem wan and are swept away in a blaze of synonyms. The writer reaches for baubles, instead of relying on eyes, ears and insight, and unfortunately the baubles are the common property of the tribe. (Political writers slogging through a long, repetitive campaign face similar temptations. In fact, sports clichés are freely imported into politics: You read of the frontrunner in a crowded field stumbling in a crucial primary while a dark horse is closing so fast that the convention will go right down to the wire.)

Second, some writers still treat sports as a mystical saga of superheroes, untainted by the ordinary grit and grime of human endeavor. That approach doesn't foster understatement. (Great sportswriters often have a soft spot for the more marginal athletes, who make it to the major leagues—barely—on effort and determination rather than an abundance of natural ability.)

Finally, there is the linguistic cannibalism in the closely knit world of sports, where writers, editors, coaches, athletic directors, players and publicists keep steady company and recklessly borrow from the sports pages and each other. As Walker said, "Some of these words and phrases were pithy and effective. The trouble was that when one writer hit upon a good phrase the others took it up and used it until it became threadbare." The chewing of communal cud still produces a stream of new clichés every week without abandoning the old.

A crescendo builds with the fatuous questions and prefabricated answers at recurrent rituals: the locker room quotes, the pre-game and post-game meditations of coaches, the profound speculations of managers about World Series prospects ("We'll just have to score more runs than they do").

There was a college football coach with a perennially losing team who had a card file with trite quotations that he consulted when talking to reporters. It's a wonder more of them don't, considering the bright sayings that keep tumbling into print:

> We just want the Eagles to respect us. They're playing for pride. If we can control the ball, we'll win. You've got to give them credit. We lost the momentum in the second half. Nobody can afford turnovers. They're a very physical team.

Writers are condemned to the cliché treadmill not by their subject matter, but by mental indolence. Red Smith wrote sports for nearly half a century until his death in 1982, but in his latter years you'd find fewer clichés in his copy than there are snakes in Ireland. "I have tried to become simpler, straighter and more pure in my language," he once said. "I look at some of the stuff I wrote in the past and I say, 'Gee, I should have cooled it a little more.' "

The writer who finds himself drifting toward the hotter latitudes, not to say the cliché doldrums, should cool it a little more.

We would then have fewer leads that tell us that "the Minnesota Vikings want to avoid home-grown players like the plague" or that baseball manager Jeff Torborg "has insisted all along—one game at a time." Or even:

The Los Angeles Dodgers' pennant hopes are still full speed ahead even though they are stuck in reverse.

"We've got our backs to the wall. . ."

A fairly neat trick which, incidentally, did not win them the pennant.

And we'd see more leads like this:

The new model of the Big Red Machine won with spare parts. The Cincinnati Reds were so good in this World Series that they lost two-thirds of their starting outfield Saturday night and still swept the Oakland Athletics.

Perhaps some day we'll no longer see *athleticism, velocity, speed merchant, give their best shot, paint the corner, ring his bell, showed lots of heart, garnered* (goals, baskets, points), *collected wins, extended their skein, down to the wire, legendary* (anybody in the Hall of Fame), *romp, blast* (home run), *return artists*. But don't hold your breath.

Fifty years ago, Walker laid it out:

The sports reading public today is remarkably well informed. It cannot be tickled by mere extravagance of writing. A lazy and incompetent writer finds it increasingly difficult to get by with a sloppy story, spun on a thread of artificial conceits. The demand is that he give his readers the facts, and give them straight. When crowds of 75,000 and more attend baseball and football games, and boxing matches, while millions more are listening on the radio, the sports writer should realize that he has an immense, well-informed audience that does not like to be fooled or short-changed.

And that was long before television increased the audience that could not only hear, but see for itself.

The Overreachers

Many clichés are metaphors and similes that have been worked to death but refused decent burial. Expert writers fluently devise their own, which helps make their language concrete and "pictureable." But there are perils, too, in groping for novelties, and tyros tend to overreach themselves. Figures of speech are slippery characters, valuable when they're on target, distracting when they misfire.

The apt figure of speech has remarkable power; an example is Saul Pett's phrase that New York's baldish mayor Ed Koch "blushed like a kosher pumpkin," and, in a different vein, Jules Loh's metaphor in describing the arrival of a white whooping crane in a flight of drab sand cranes: "As the formation winged past the curtain of a mountain, the whooper appeared as a single glistening pearl in a pale gray strand."

Splendid images. Try for such phrases, but don't try too hard; a strained figure of speech is usually ludicrous, dismal or both.

In fact, when you're aglow with satisfaction over a newly hatched, unusual figure, give it a clinical second look. Such caution would have saved some embarrassment in the following newspaper examples:

Interest rates are sprouting fresh skids today.

In a financial hothouse?

His eyebrows followed in a tempestuous stare.

Most people stare, non-tempestuously, with their eyes.

Frustration, skepticism and humor juggled for the upper hand yesterday for those whose international odysseys were to have begun at the TWA terminal.

Quite a little carnival, but frustration, skepticism and humor are abstractions that don't juggle, and even jugglers don't juggle for the upper hand. The writer may have meant *jostle*, but that wouldn't help much, either.

Metaphors: Mixed and Protracted

Mixed metaphors are common misdemeanors:

While the controversy is the latest storm to engulf him, it is the latest chapter in a long series of tangled events.

These are clichés, but a storm doesn't turn into a chapter.

A dead metaphor is sometimes brought to unseemly life by an active one:

It was a rooted idea and it ran away with them.

Not unless you uproot it first.

His neighborhood, nestled east of Grand Concourse and south of Fordham Road, while remaining a *womb* of friends, family and fellow Italian-Americans, has suffered from police layoffs, an increase in burglaries, and the destruction or abandonment of apartment buildings.

A womb generally doesn't nestle, though something is said to nestle in a womb. Worse, we're dealing with a giant and hyperactive womb.

Metaphors are sprinters, not long-distance runners. Know when to let go:

Smith, an avid sailor, has been at the helm of his company five years, and during that time has steered it past many shoals.

The worst squall he faced was a bitter proxy fight, but he weathered it and the seas have been calm since.

In fact, the only one who makes waves now is Smith himself.

By the third paragraph, the reader needs a life preserver. Here's another protracted metaphor that should have been tackled before reaching the third graf:

CHARLOTTESVILLE, Va.—For the University of Virginia's enthusiastic but inexperienced offensive linemen, the first weeks of the college football season will represent trial by fire.

Will the searing heat of pressurized competition vaporize their pride and melt their competitive instincts, the way it did with their predecessors?

Or will it instead transform them into a strong, resilient alloy? Their coaches and teammates are anxiously awaiting an answer—for the success or failure of the offensive line will likely determine whether the Cavaliers' season glows brightly or soon flickers into unfulfilled darkness.

The Personification Peril

Personification, with allegory, was the literary rage in the 18th century, but it goes against the modern grain and today is the feeblest of metaphorical devices. Language itself, of course, personifies: We say that luck smiles, fate frowns, and the like. But this is unobtrusive. Not so when we trot out Old Man Winter, Father Time, Mother Nature and endow them with human traits.

Destiny's finger was about to tickle this man.

Winter thrust his icy fist into the nation's mid-section today.
He was riding high until Dame Fortune turned a cold shoulder.
The mercury struggled all day to climb above zero.

Frankly, my friends, the mercury doesn't give a damn.
Writing like this was on the wane when the weather service
gave it fresh impetus with its disastrous decision to christen hurri-
canes. Some writers have found the temptation irresistible. Here's
a milder example of what's done to our frolicsome tempests:

> The petticoat of hurricane Belle sashayed through New Jersey toward
> a landfall on Long Island today, buckling a four-block section of Atlan-
> tic City's famed boardwalk . . .

Actually, if anything sashayed it was Belle rather than her
boardwalk-buckling petticoats, but it doesn't really matter.

Other Poisonous Mixtures

We've been considering verbal mishaps that shouldn't happen,
but that carry no grievous consequences. It's different when, in
chasing too hard after a clever, cute or poetic expression, a writer
comes up with an incongruous analogy. Don't mix the important
with the trivial, the serious with the silly. The brew can explode.

> BALTIMORE—The smoke has cleared from the Vatican's Sistine
> chapel, but the fire still smolders in the locker room of the troubled
> Baltimore Colts.

Equating a papal election with the intramural squabbles of a
football team may be an original thought, but one that should have
been stillborn.

> Then again, trying to find people who quit smoking for the day in the
> tobacco company's headquarters ranked right up there with soliciting
> for a birth control clinic in the Vatican.

An editor commenting on this passage in the paper's in-house
bulletin said: "Hot stuff, maybe, for *Saturday Night Live*. Humor
in news and feature stories has its limits. Being gratuitously clever
and flippant about religious tenets exceeds those limits."

> SLIPPERY ROCK, Pa. (AP)—Slippery Rock University Coach Bob
> DiSpirito doesn't worry his back-up kicker will improvise an ill-

advised pass at an inopportune time, as Garo Yepremian once did in a Super Bowl.

Bonnie West, you see, has no arms. Heart, yes; arms, no.

SOUTH BERWICK, Maine (AP)—A man who caught an Atlantic sturgeon roughly the size of basketball great Wilt Chamberlain had the fish seized by the state, and could be sentenced to a year in prison and fined $1,000.

The fish, at 7-feet-8-inches, was 6 inches longer than Chamberlain, and outweighed him by 25 pounds during the basketball star's playing prime.

The moral is obvious. Don't reach. Keep your critical faculties awake. Does this parallel make sense? Is that comparison far-fetched? That humorous sally offensive? The metaphor mixed? The simile comparing apples with oranges? Is it perhaps just a decorative cliché?

When in doubt, strike it out. Even apt figures of speech should be used sparingly; too many create a filigree that's out of place in the simple, direct style. As Strunk and White note in *The Elements of Style*, similes coming in rapid fire weary readers by asking them to compare everything with something else.

Words to Swear At

These clichés are among the dreariest in captivity, in one editor's opinion anyway. The list is not exhaustive. You may not find your favorite here:

armed to the teeth	burn one's bridges
banker's hours	burn the midnight oil
battle royal	burning issue
beat a hasty retreat	bury the hatchet
beauty and the beast	calm before the storm
bewildering variety	cherished belief
beyond the shadow of a doubt	clear the decks
bite the dust	club-wielding police
blazing inferno	colorful scene
blessed event	conspicuous by its absence
blessing in disguise	coveted award
blissful ignorance	crack troops
bull in a china shop	curvaceous blonde

dramatic new move
dread disease
dream come true
drop in the bucket
fame and fortune
feast or famine
fickle fortune
gentle hint
glaring omission
glutton for punishment
gory details
grief-stricken
Grim Reaper
hand in glove
hammer out (an agreement)
happy couple
hook, line and sinker
head over heels in love
heart of gold
heavily armed troops
iron out (problems)
intensive investigation
Lady Luck
lash out
last-ditch stand
leave no stone unturned
leaps and bounds
light at the end of the tunnel
lightning speed
limp into port
lock, stock and barrel
long arm of coincidence
   (the law)
man in the street
marvels of science
matrimonial bliss (knot)
meager pension
miraculous escape
Mother Nature
move into high gear
never a dull moment
Old Man Winter
paint a grim picture

pay the supreme penalty
picture of health
pillar of (the church, society)
pinpoint the cause
police dragnet
pool of blood
posh resort
powder keg
pre-dawn darkness
prestigious law firm
proud heritage
proud parents
pursuit of excellence
radiant bride
red faces, red-faced
reins of government
rushed to the scene
scantily clad
scintilla of evidence
scurried to shelter
selling like hotcakes
spearheading the campaign
spirited debate
spotlessly clean
sprawling base, facility
spreading like wildfire
steaming jungle
stick out like a sore thumb
stranger than fiction
storm of protest
supreme sacrifice
surprise move
sweep under the rug
sweet harmony
sweetness and light
tempest in a teapot
tender mercies
terror-stricken
tip of the iceberg
tower of strength
trail of death and destruction
true colors
vanish in thin air

walking encyclopedia
wealth of information
whirlwind campaign

wouldn't touch with a 10-foot
    pole
last but not least

Doubleheaders

Lawyers love paired words with related meanings, like *null and void, part and parcel, aid and abet, sum and substance, irrelevant and immaterial*. They're kissing cousins of redundancies.

Leave such sing-song pleasures to the barristers. When a doubleheader comes to you unbidden, as it usually does, pause to consider if one word won't say it all:

beck and call
betwixt and between
bits and pieces
blunt and brutal
bound and determined
clear and simple
confused and bewildered
disgraced and dishonored
each and every
fair and just

few and far between
nervous and distraught
nook and cranny
pick and choose
ready and willing
right and proper
safe and sound
shy and withdrawn
smooth and silky
various and sundry

FEATURES: A View From the Poets' Corner

11

The hard news story marches briskly through the whats, whens, wheres, looking neither right nor left, packing in enough details to give readers a clear picture.

In features, the immediacy of the event is secondary. The plain ladder of descending news values is replaced by human interest, mood, atmosphere, emotion, irony, humor. Features aim to give readers pleasure and entertainment along with (and, on the fluffier side, sometimes in lieu of) information.

The range of features encompasses the gourmet column and Orphaned Dog of the Week as well as news enterprise of major significance. The more compelling features supplement the straight news content in timely and topical ways: they illuminate events, offer perspective, explanation and interpretation, record trends, tell people about people.

Because features are less shackled to the moment than hard news stories, writers usually have more time. Proper use of that time takes a special discipline. Some writers, unfortunately, use it to lard their copy with clusters of adjectives, purple passages and other decorative devices. If you feel the decorative impulse coming on, lie down until it goes away. Strong feature writing is simple, clear, orderly, free of labored mannerisms and tricks that call attention to the writing itself rather than the substance.

First, the Beginning

Most hard news stories follow a basic pattern. By comparison, the feature floats free. The writer has the choice of many approaches. This offers splendid opportunities to the skilled and imaginative, but it also holds traps for the unwary, particularly in the first several paragraphs, the intro.

There's never any doubt about the point of a straight news story; the lead tells you. In features, that point may be postponed. You don't have to play it out explicitly in the first graf or two. But readers need to know soon what the story is about, and why they should go on reading. Bury this crucial point too far beneath anecdote, description and atmospherics, and you'll exasperate readers rather than intrigue them. This is what happened in the following story:

> Come right in. Dinner will be ready in just a minute. Susie is making dinner tonight. You can hear her in the kitchen, talking to Connie Karli, who is in charge here.
>
> That's Connie's voice, telling Susie to make sure that none of the eggshells get into the bowl. Tonight, it's scrambled eggs, sausage and salad. It's slow going, with Connie steadily supervising.
>
> "You have to be careful with the shells," Connie says.
>
> "Why, Connie?" Susie asks, scrupulously scooping out eggshells with a fork. "Why do you have to be careful with the shells?"
>
> Susie is very cautious when she cooks; she takes great delight in serving a good meal, when it's over, but what she likes best is setting the table. Susie, who is 35, with dark hair and delicate skin, never cooked when she lived at home with her parents, but now she takes her turn making dinner.
>
> Since everyone moved in at 366 Highland Ave. the only major renovations have been in the kitchen, which is now filled with new appliances . . .

The story continues for another long paragraph before readers are told they're visiting a home for the mentally retarded. Maybe some guessed, but more were probably wondering when the writer would get to the point.

The following intro sets a scene descriptively, but rambles through massed adjectives and generalities.

HATTERAS, N.C.—The narrow road that threads its way northward along Hatteras Island from Hatteras Inlet to the village of Nags Head has been called one of America's most scenic drives.

To the east, white-capped waves roll in from what early mariners knew as "The Graveyard of the Atlantic." Pamlico Sound, dotted with scores of fishing boats, sparkles to the west. Flocks of wild ducks and long-legged exotic birds perch on the high dunes along the road to Cape Hatteras National Seashore and Pea Island Wildlife Refuge.

In the winter, the Outer Banks region is isolated except for the hardy native fishermen. Tourists don't venture onto the storm-swept islands until the summer warms up the 75 miles of beaches and the dozens of motels and restaurants open for the season.

Readers must plod through two more paragraphs of this travel-brochure prose until they are told that the "scenic and historic" Outer Banks, like other barrier islands, are threatened by erosion, the sea and the carelessness of man.

Equally unfortunate, the writer doesn't offer a single fresh observation of the wild beauties of the place but falls back on clustered adjectives: *scenic, historic, white-capped, storm-swept, hardy, exotic*—words trotted out automatically for such occasions.

Next, the start of a piece on artificial life by AP Special Correspondent Nancy Shulins. She delays the transition to her main subject until the seventh graf, but it works because from the outset the reader is lured into an uncanny world that points in that direction:

It's a dog-eat-dog world inside Danny Hillis' computer, home to 64,000 competing programs. Only the fittest will survive.

Fitness, in this 5-foot universe, is the ability to sort letters alphabetically. But Hillis, its creator, doesn't teach his programs how to sort. Instead, he sets up a world in which programs with sorting ability are more likely to survive. Then he waits.

The early programs are terrible sorters. The worst are killed off right away. Some put A before Z by blind luck, but that's good enough. They "mate," merging successful traits in "offspring" that do better still.

Evolution proceeds at a dizzying pace. The result, after 10,000 generations: "A better program for alphabetical sorting than anything I could write," says Hillis, a programmer with a doctorate from Massachusetts Institute of Technology.

There can be no doubt that software that evolved in Hillis' computer is superior to anything a human can produce.

The question is, is it alive?

Probably not—or as Hillis is apt to answer, not yet. But to him and other scientists on the frontier known as artificial life, it's only a matter of time before life becomes—literally—what we make of it.

Following is another anecdotal approach, from *The Wall Street Journal*. This intro, too, leads straight to the subject:

LONDON—A year before he was overwhelmingly voted out of office as prime minister of Jamaica, Michael Manley gave a testimonial to his alma mater.

"The London School of Economics," he wrote, "had a profound influence on my early development. I find to this day that some of the habits of thought and analysis which I acquired at LSE are useful, some 30 years later."

Mr. Manley, an ardent Socialist, was widely blamed for the collapse of his country's economy. The London School of Economics, founded by the Fabians, is just as widely blamed for educating people like Mr. Manley in the ideals of British Socialism—its own invention—and sending them off to make a mess of the Third World.

At the end of the third (seductive) graf, the reader is firmly on course—and hooked. His interest is whetted. That is all a good feature intro need do. The significant elements of the story can be left for later. Here are the next two grafs, building toward a nice surprise:

With a reputation like that, it may seem fitting that the LSE is finally getting its financial comeuppance. It is suffering more than almost any other university in Britain as Margaret Thatcher's monetarist government hacks away at the supposed excesses of higher education in the welfare state. There is, however, an anomaly in this. British monetarism, it seems, is an LSE invention as well.

Much as Michael Manley's reputation may have been deserved, the LSE's is not. "It's one of the most bewildering things about being at LSE," says Ralf Dahrendorf, the German scholar and politician who became its director in 1974.

The school, renowned as a Socialist breeding ground, actually harbors what may be the most right-wing department of government in the West.

The last two paragraphs are important, indeed the "hard" substance of the story, but nothing was lost working up to them slowly. The writer could, of course, have started the piece like this:

LONDON—The London School of Economics, reputed to be a propagator of Socialist ideas through its alumni in the Third World, actually harbors what may be the most right-wing department of government in the West.

That would seem acceptable as far as it goes, but flat and dry in comparison with the anecdotal, storytelling method the writer chose. This, of course, is the special appeal of the feature story.

The Interest Is *Human*

One problem with the dehydrated lead is that it is general. Moving from the general to the particular is seldom as effective in feature writing as the other way around. A broad-brush opener tends to be duller, unless the writer is unusually lucky or adroit. Whenever possible, raise the curtain on a human actor and human action, not a juiceless stage setting.

If, for example, you start a report on the effects of the Cuban influx on Miami with an "overview" of the emigrés' influence on the city's economy, culture and politics, you're likely to wind up with an abstract catalog that lacks human interest.

If, on the other hand, you start with an anecdote about an individual or family whose experience exemplifies one or more of these phenomena, the readers are instantly caught up in somebody's life. They'll follow that with greater interest than a parade of Issues and Problems.

Good feature writers capitalize on this and bring it off even where a particularized, human-interest focus seems hard to devise. Following is the beginning of a story by Saul Pett on the federal bureaucracy, an 8,500-word blockbuster that dealt with the size, pervasiveness and complexity of the government, how it got that way and with what mixed results—a story done well enough to win a Pulitzer Prize for Pett.

Technically, it is a masterful intro, piquing the reader's interest at every turn by foreshadowing with specifics all the main elements of a singularly complicated story.

WASHINGTON (AP)—We begin with the sentiments of two Americans two centuries apart but joined in a symmetry of indignation.

One said this: "He has erected a multitude of offices and sent hither swarms of officers to harass our people, and eat out their substance."

The other said this: "The government drives me nuts. The forms are so complicated I have to call my accountant at $35 an hour and my lawyer at $125 an hour just to get a translation."

The latter opinion belongs to Roger Gregory, a carpenter and small contractor from Sandy Springs, Md., a man of otherwise genial disposition. The first statement was made by Thomas Jefferson, in the Declaration of Independence, in the bill of particulars against the king of England that launched the American Revolution.

It is one of the ironies of history that a nation born out of a deep revulsion for large, overbearing government is now itself complaining, from sea to shining sea, about large, overbearing government.

Somewhere between Thomas Jefferson and Roger Gregory, something went awry with our American growth hormone. And now in our 40th presidency, Ronald Reagan is trying to saddle and tame a brontosaurus of unimaginable size, ubiquity and complexity.

In designing a government, James Madison said, "The great difficulty is this: You must first control the governed and, in the next place, oblige it to govern itself." Has it?

Several things are noteworthy about this intro. With 8,200 words still to follow, the first three grafs, with the use of particulars, set the reader on a firm course. And when Pett moves from the particular to the general, the irony of the nation complaining about overbearing government, the main theme of the story is clear.

The next two paragraphs invite the reader's question: How did it happen? Why? These are answered in what follows. It is a remarkable success in particularizing an intro on a whopping abstraction like the federal establishment.

No Precooked Dinners

The news story starts from an event. The feature story starts from an idea. "Let's do a story on the changes in Appalachia," the editor decides. "There haven't been any changes," the reporter discovers. "Fine, then let's do a story on why not. After all, the government poured millions into the place."

This is vague, but that's how it should be. Refining and massaging the idea is the outcome of, not the preliminary to, reporting. Neither you nor your editor can know in advance where the scent will lead you. It may go in unexpected directions. Writers who start with a detailed blueprint may have to tear it up, wasting time and energy. Some, God forbid, even prefabricate a lead or an intro. This is a form of prejudgment that handicaps you in two ways. First, you will restrict your reporting from the outset to sources and material that fit your preconceived thesis. You may miss a far better angle. Second, and worse, you may miss what's really important and thereby distort the truth.

Start your reporting and interviewing with an open mind. In time, and by dint of legwork and research, the story will assume a natural shape. You may have wanted, say, to do the Appalachian piece from the perspective of state officials and welfare workers who ladle out government aid. You may find that three old ladies who were among the first food stamp recipients, all of whose children worked in the mines, can open up richer vistas. The point is, stay loose until you have enough of a feel to decide that you have the right theme. At that phase, you'll be able to narrow your reporting to its requirements.

At first, though, cast your net wide. You never know what facts and details, peripheral when you haul them in, will turn into treasure when you write. The fact that the mine inspector is a rose fancier is worth little—until you discover that the mine operator he's dragged to court shares the floral passion and has been bested twice by the inspector in a state flower show. You won't get such piquant detail, which gives your story vitality, unless your questions and your curiosity range well beyond the reservation of the immediate subject.

Since you'll need to reconstruct a scene, recapture mood and atmosphere, you might do well to follow the cherished practice of AP's Hugh Mulligan, a longtime feature writer turned columnist: "I find it helpful to copy down emotions, observations and passing thoughts on how I feel about what I'm witnessing or hearing, mainly because I may never feel that way again when I sit down to write," he has said. "I take endless notes on everything I hear and see and smell and think or moon about."

Because most good feature writers amass a far greater hoard of material for every enterprise than they can use, writing becomes a great winnowing. Writers often can't bear to part with an anecdote, a character vignette, or a nosegay of facts that are amusing and interesting. But do they bear directly on the subject? If not, show them the door. Your profile of the single-minded engineer deals with his astonishing labors and the qualities of an infinitely precise mind that bring them about. His mother-in-law's odd experiences at a haunted house in Scotland are beguiling, but beside the point. Get rid of them. If you have three anecdotes illustrating the engineer's strange work habits, from midnight to eight in the morning, use the *one* that best makes the point. Don't belabor it with the others, however charming.

(As an example of a profile that gets its man with great economy of style, with all of its anecdotes and incidents strictly advancing its theme, read AP Special Correspondent Jules Loh's 600-word story on Big Six Henderson at the end of this chapter.)

This process of selection is the feature writer's purgatory. The good ones go through it with every story, though never cheerfully. How far the winnowing proceeds also depends on the editor's ukase on available space. Rebellions over such matters are not unheard of, but reasonable restrictions of wordage, besides being an inescapable fact of newspaper life, are a challenge rather than an inhibition. As Don Murray, former Boston newspaperman, now an English professor at the University of New Hampshire, put it: "Creativity is not the product of freedom, but the product of the conflict between freedom and discipline." The true craftsman can paint on a small canvas as fetchingly as on a large one.

Much agony can ensue from a craving to be definitive, which isn't the same as being thorough. Journalists, including feature writers, can never hope to say the last word on any subject. If you try that on a topic like nuclear power, or desegregation, or the genetic factor in intelligence, you're assailing Everest with your forehead. Limit yourself to a manageable slice of the subject. Your contribution will be the more valuable for it.

A feature story needs structure. Like the Red River, it can take all sorts of bends and curves, but it always stays within the banks.

No offshoots flow from it. Readers should be able to follow it as if in a canoe, always curious about what's around the next bend.

Chronological Approach

Chronological narrative, which kept Scheherazade alive, is the simplest structure and often remarkably effective, particularly in reconstructing large events like the Mount St. Helens eruption or the dark drama of the Peoples Temple.

While many features include chunks of chronology, it is usually modified by various devices. You may start in the middle of an action and use flashbacks. Always, you should spice straight chronology with foreshadowings—teasers, hints of what lies around the bend.

In a story on the 100th anniversary of Franklin D. Roosevelt's birth, for instance, Pett gave a largely chronological account of the president's mighty labors. But he framed the narrative in the experiences of two plain citizens whose lives had been greatly changed by the New Deal. (Direct tie-in with the present is a good practice in stories on historical subjects.) His format also gave Pett a human interest intro, leading from the two individuals to the affairs of state, and an ironic ending: one of those old New Dealers' sons had voted for Reagan.

Structure need not be elaborate. You can build some stories from scenes, more or less connected, with or without narrative transitions, each highlighting a significant episode. The "reporter's notebook" technique is a pleasant variant, informal and chatty, dipping rather than digging into a subject. It usually consists of separate items and vignettes, sketching various aspects of a place or event. The result can be highly readable, but success depends on sharp observation and good detail. And the pearls should be on a common strand, with some thematic relation among the items; you're not cleaning out the attic.

AP's Sid Moody devised a novel structure for a profile of New Jersey. The story was a dazzling almanac of facts—historical, contemporary, statistical, out-of-the-way, plainly odd—interspersed at times with non-facts by way of humorous hyperbole. The format was a drive along the New Jersey Turnpike, with Moody as the genial tour director, pausing at each exit to display the economic, physical and social landscape.

Here's how he began the story:

N.J. TURNPIKE (AP)— Standup comic: "Swine flu was discovered in New Jersey—where else?" (Laughter.)

Other Comic: "The Mafia is feeling the recession. They laid off four judges in Jersey." (More laughter.)

New Jersey today is an automatic boff, funnier than Brooklyn or downtown Burbank. The laughter emanates from the trillions of non-Jerseyans who cruise up the Turnpike staring at rear bumpers, dodging chemical trucks, sniffing refineries and gladly surrendering $1.50 to escape across the Hudson into New York.

It gets no respect. Yet Jersey gave America the steam locomotive (Hoboken, 1825); baseball (same place, 1846); football (New Brunswick, 1869); Edison's lightbulb (Menlo Park, 1879); movie cliffhangers (Palisades, early 1900s); the four-lane highway and cloverleaf (Newark); Count Basie; Valium; Meryl Streep; Allen Ginsberg; me and Secaucus. (Laughter.) And it may become a pioneer in what to do, and what not to do, about rotted cities, dwindling farmland, aging suburbs, regional planning and local government. It may just be where the country is going.

New Jersey is 7.3 million people; 5 zillion pickups; sixth among the states in per capita income; 300-plus garbage dumps with Jimmy Hoffa buried in every one; 150,000 deer; 12 armored divisions of Mafiosi; nine casinos; 16 skillion suburbs; 3,518 bartenders named Louie; one covered bridge; two U.S. senators, one a basketball player, the other convicted in the Abscam affair, and 40 of the state variety, three of them indicted. All of this acted out on a small stage.

A peek at the future? Turn off here, Exit 1.

Yup, that's a silo. We have 9,100 farms with about 1 million acres. They produce $2,977 per acre, tops in the nation. But half the farmland is owned by non-farmers. Read developers. Jersey farmers, average age 53, have a morale problem with subdivisions crowding right into the barnyard. The new suburbanites complain about chicken feathers on the front lawns, about missing trains because they got stuck behind an 8 mph tractor. The Garden State grows only 54 percent of its vegetables. Milk comes from Wisconsin. The farmers sell out and retire to Florida.

Belatedly, New Jersey thinks this is no solution.

Without following Moody all the way to Exit 9, you might note two things:

1. An avalanche of facts and figures doesn't necessarily smother a reader. Moody's cornucopia gives his piece a special charm. Moody (a persistent, if flawed, trombonist on the side) is aware that sometimes there is music in mathematical preciseness.

2. The fifth paragraph performs a valuable service, crystallizing the significance of the story by relating New Jersey's condition to the nation at large. All sizable features benefit from such a "pregnant paragraph" high in the story, telling the reader: "Here's what's important (or unusual) about the story. Read on."

You may have caught Moody sneaking in a first person pronoun ("me and Secaucus"). Fine for this occasion as another humorous aside. But in general, leave the perpendicular pronoun to the columnists. The exceptions are rare—stories in which the writer tells about an expressly personal experience, perhaps overcoming a debilitating illness or surviving three weeks in the Amazon garlanded with anacondas.

People are by definition human interest, or at least human, and profiles are a staple of feature output. They range from the full-fledged portrait of 2,000 words to more cursory sketches of someone in the news.

Don't cram a profile with routine biographical detail; keep that for the obit. Look for the characteristics, habits, traits, working methods and experiences that make your subject different.

In short profiles of "personalities in the news," it's a good idea to concentrate on qualities that got them there. If you're dealing with a person who's just ascended to high office in a major corporation, pick anecdotes, quotes and background details that help explain the success.

When you can, relate details and color to the main theme: *She picks her clothes with the discriminating eye developed in six years as the company's leading buyer. In her gardening—her main avocation—she's as organized and meticulous as she's said to be in running the new division.*

Routine profile interviews of celebrities tend to be the least promising. That's because celebrities are acutely media-conscious, forever intent on their, Lord help them, "image." They have stock answers to all the usual questions and become vague or tongue-tied at unusual ones. They like people. They think the city they're in is wonderful. They like sports. They like music. They like babies. They like mothers. They think love is wonderful. They adore walking in the rain. They find everything a challenge. They are, in fact, animated clichés.

The only hope is to get such people to talk about their one vein of expertise or enthusiasm, if any; the actress may be interesting on acting techniques, the schlock author on how he trip-hammers his epics together.

The value of steering people in interviews to subjects with which they have real affinity and thorough familiarity is often overlooked. Ask a plumber or a microbiologist about politics, theology or current affairs, and you'll usually get regurgitated opinions as fascinating as the telephone book.

Let them discourse about the ins and outs of plumbing or microbiology and they're apt to wax voluble, enthusiastic and downright informative. Such stuff, even when slightly technical, usually is interesting even to readers without passion for pipe wrenches or electron microscopes.

Profiles of Very Important Citizens often require great effort to avoid the puffery fed you by the handiest sources—assorted aides, associates, flunkeys. Tapping Wilbur Lickspittle Jr. for quotes about his boss, Jarvis Housingstart, the Biggest Builder in the West, is unlikely to prove revealing. Balancing Lickspittle's fawning testimonial with the bleats of tenants at Housingstart Heights, where the roof recently blew off in a mild breeze, won't necessarily get you closer to the real Housingstart. You need sources who know him well but are neither beholden nor harbor a vendetta. It takes work.

Where Solemnity Palls

A sense of humor, an eye for irony, and a light touch are formidable assets. You're thrice blessed if you have them. Not every subject can be treated lightly, but none calls for stodgy solemnity. The feature, after all, is intended to please as well as inform. A certain playfulness of style is seldom out of place. Pett's epic on the bureaucracy, as you saw from the earlier sample, was relaxed and informal for all of its weightiness of subject.

Here's another example of Pett in full cry:

NEW YORK (AP)—He is the freshest thing to blossom in New York since chopped liver, a mixed metaphor of a politician, the antithesis of the packaged leader, irrepressible, candid, impolitic, spontaneous, funny, feisty, independent, uncowed by voter blocs, unsexy, unhandsome, unfashionable and altogether charismatic, a man oddly at peace with himself in an unpeaceful place, a mayor who presides over the country's largest Babel with unseemly joy.

Clearly, an original. Asked once what his weaknesses were, Ed Koch said that for the life of him he couldn't think of any. "I like myself," he said.

The streets are still dirty. The subways are still unsafe. The specter of bankruptcy is never further away than next year's loan. But Edward Irwin Koch, who runs the place like a Jewish mother with no fear of the rich relatives, appears to be the most popular mayor of this implausible town since Fiorello LaGuardia more than a generation ago.

Yes, yes, elsewhere I extol the short sentence and especially the short lead, and this one runs 65 words. Which only means that when a good writer breaks a rule for good reason, it works. Anyway, the reader is having fun.

Poetic License Forbidden

Feature writing, as that lead demonstrates, offers greater latitude than straight news writing. It thrives on color, nuance, wit, fancy, emotive words, dialogue, character. Feature writers, like novelists, have many literary devices to engage readers emotionally, and that's their privilege.

But freedom, as has often been noted, entails responsibility. Feature writers must be accurate and scrupulously fair.

What you say happened must have happened in precisely that way. Frolic with words, enjoy yourself (if any writer can), but remember there's no poetic or literary license when it comes to facts. Repeat that to yourself every morning.

Fairness is more difficult to pinpoint, but a person can be sandbagged in many ways by the techniques in the feature writer's armory—through selection of details, through invidious description, through the use of adjectives and even through the setting of a scene.

That doesn't mean that every anecdote that presents a subject in an unfavorable light must be balanced by a favorable one, or that every critical comment must be offset by a burst of praise. Fairness is not a matter of arithmetic.

It does mean that feature writers, as honest reporters, recognize that life is multi-dimensional, that motives are often ambiguous, that moral judgments are beyond their purview, that a one-sided portrayal, whether of a person or an institution, is a sin even less pardonable than shoddy technique.

Artists at Work

The best way to learn feature writing, or any writing, is to read—study—the work of those who know their business. I've drawn heavily on some of them in this section.

What follows is a small selection of features that repay reading and illustrate some of the points discussed. I wish space permitted a fuller representation.

The first is a story by the late Hal Boyle, irreplaceable dean of the AP Poets' Corner, reporter, Pulitzer Prize winner, war correspondent, columnist, master of the simple declarative sentence. The story is about the birth and death of a calf. Technically, it is a fine example of the power of understatement and of precise visual detail.

The second is a short profile of a retired revenue agent, by Jules Loh. It is obvious from the chosen material that Loh could have written at twice the length; he chose a smaller canvas. Note the economy of language. Every sentence is pertinent to the theme, every word tells.

The third is by AP Special Correspondent Tad Bartimus. It was a difficult assignment: to interview and write about people staggered by a recent bereavement. Moreoever, this was written under some time pressure.

They represent different categories of features, but note what all three have in common. Each is free of mannerisms, verbal flourishes, literary tinsel. Each demonstrates the unassailable essential: good feature writing proceeds from good reporting.

Read and enjoy.

LIFE AND DEATH IN A COW BARN
By Hal Boyle

LONG VALLEY, N.J. (AP)—It was an ordinary Sunday outside the big, cool dairy barn. The dressed-up people came and went to church, the less dressed up people from the city enjoyed the sunny country-side.

Inside the big, cool dairy barn it was even more of an ordinary day. Cows have no Sunday. The daily drama of life and death among the herd went on unchanged except for one thing.

There was a young girl present who saw the drama for the first time. The events of the day changed her, perhaps forever. The three cows involved were numbered 204 and 140 and 219—and the first was old and through, the second was young and having her first calf, and the third was middle-aged and having maybe her third or fourth calf.

No. 204 was at the head of the barn and lying, too weary to get up, at the front of the barn with her head in its stanchion. She was 14, very old for a cow. Her milk had fleshed a thousand distant children she had never seen. But now she lay there, unprotestingly, waiting for the slaughterer's truck to come and take her away.

During the morning, No. 140, the young heifer, delivered her first calf after a rugged ordeal. Worn out by the struggle and oblivious to the responsibilities of motherhood, she wandered away from her sprawling, weak, tan calf.

A group of summer residents who came down to see the calf found that No. 219, the middle-aged cow, had taken up the duties of the confused young mother. She was carefully and methodically cleaning the sprawling calf with her tongue, as animals do.

Suddenly it became apparent the middle-aged cow's own ordeal of maternity was at hand. One of the men turned to a young girl, his niece, and said:

"If you're going to get back to the city before the traffic ties you up, you'd better leave now."

"I've never seen anything born before," she said. "I want to stay."

"But it may be hours," he said. "You can't tell."

"Just for a little while," she pleaded. "Then I'll be off."

Her uncle and the others left and the young girl was alone in the filtered light of the barn, sweet with the deep rich scent of hay and animal bodies. Old cow No. 204, a factory worn out, glanced at her with the idle and placid disinterest of age.

The young girl knelt beside No. 219. The miracle of approaching birth made the two one. She knit her fingers and tugged at them tensely in unconscious rhythm with the laboring cow.

"Please," she whispered. "Try again, harder."

All at once they were three—or almost three. The calf was half-born. Then something was wrong.

"Please, please, please!" cried the girl. She heard a noise. Two dairy hands had come into the far end of the dairy barn.

"Quick!" she cried. "The calf is strangling."

The two men ran up. One grabbed a rope. With it they completed the rough obstetrics of the farm, and the calf was delivered, its forehooves raised to its muzzle in the posture of prayer.

The calf lay there—warm, wet and motionless. One workman bent and wiped its muzzle to clear the nostrils, then massaged its ribs in an attempt at artifical respiration. The calf lay still.

"But I saw its eyes move," said the girl. "If I could have called you in time . . ."

The rough workmen looked at her, puzzled. A calf is $20, more or less, and they come often on a big dairy farm.

"I don't think so," said one of the men, not unkindly.

"These things happen, you know."

As one of the men dragged the dead calf away, mother cow No. 219 let out a bellow of anguish that had a human ring of despair in it, and crashed into a chain barrier. She wandered about wildly for a moment, then lowered her head and again began licking the living calf of cow No. 140, the bewildered young heifer who hadn't yet risen to the chores of motherhood.

The young girl got into her car.

"But I saw its eyes move," she said, half crying. "If I could have just . . ."

She turned the car and headed it toward the city. She had seen the sadness of death taking life at the portal of birth, and she would always remember this Sunday, just another ordinary day on a busy farm.

BIG SIX HENDERSON
By Jules Loh

LOUISVILLE, Ky. (AP)—In Kentucky's moonshine hollows, one name still strikes awe: Big Six Henderson.

Big Six Henderson busted up more stills in his time than anybody in history. If that is not so, at least it is the legend. When moonshiners talk about Big Six Henderson, the line between truth and legend blurs.

"I don't know what the record is," Big Six Henderson allowed, thinking back on his days of prowling around in alien corn.

"I know I raided more than 5,000 stills and sent more than 5,600 moonshiners to prison. You could figure it up. I've kept a copy of my daily reports for every day I was a revenue agent."

That was for a span of 28 years until he retired a few years ago, and it figures up to roughly a still every other day. The saga of Big Six Henderson, though, is hardly told in dry statistics.

The moonshiners Big Six Henderson tracked down imparted heroic dimensions to him and respected him as much as they feared him.

"Mr. Big Six," one woman said when he came to haul her husband off to jail for a third time, "we're proud to have folks know we know you." More than a few moonshiners named their children for Big Six Henderson.

One even named his mash barrel for him, painted "Big Six" on it and talked to it fondly.

"Good morning, Big Six," he said to the barrel one day. "Why don't we just run ourselves off a little batch, you and I. What do you say to that, Big Six?"

"That you're caught, Thurlow," Big Six Henderson said, stepping out of the mist.

At 75, Big Six Henderson is still impressive to behold. He is a bear of a man, 6-foot-4, with a thick bush of white hair and eyes the color of wet turquoise. His mother named him William; Big Six was the name he picked up when he was going to law school and throwing a baseball after the fashion of Christy "Big Six" Mathewson.

His career as a lawyer was as rapid as his fastball.

"My first and only case was defending a guy who broke into a warehouse. He was guilty as hell, but I got him off. I decided if I had to make a living that way I might as well be a holdup man and at least be honest about it."

There is nothing complicated about Big Six Henderson's sense of justice.

So he became a federal treasury agent, a "revenooer" as they are known in the hills, and went about it with a single-mindedness that became the stuff of myth.

Big Six Henderson can smell a still from 10 miles off. "Actually about two miles if the wind is right," Big Six Henderson corrected.

Big Six Henderson can shoot a pistol out of your hand at a hundred yards. "Well, the way that got started was by accident. I was aiming at the man's belt buckle."

It was no myth, though, that he could creep through the woods as quiet as smoke in his green raiding suit and could run like a deer for miles. Usually he didn't have to run after his quarry.

"Homer, halt!" he shouted at one fleeing moonshiner. The man froze in his tracks.

"I'm halted, Big Six, I'm halted."

He was a legend in his time, all right, and not just because of his uncanny skill and his zealotry. He also had a reputation for fair play and decent treatment of the moonshiners he caught.

"I never regarded them as doing something evil, just illegal," Big Six Henderson said, "and I never abused them." The big man thumbed through a sheaf of his faded daily reports, looking wistfully at the names.

"Killed a few, but never abused them."

BAND OF BROTHERS
By Tad Bartimus

BUCKNER, Mo. (AP)—There is so little left.

A red cardboard valentine with torn paper lace, which proclaims, "I love you Mom." A carefully penned Thanksgiving essay in which the writer says he's grateful for his family "to have someone to love me." A child's "Life Story" book with extra pages left blank for future adventures.

Chad Eugene Gragg, 12, Aaron Wayne Gragg, 11, and Stephen Douglas Gragg, 8, died together at dusk on the cold afternoon of Feb. 4.

It was Aaron's 11th birthday. Despite admonitions from a teacher and a chum who rode home with him on the bus, he chose to celebrate it by sliding on the frozen surface of a farmer's pond.

The ice broke. Aaron fell into the cold water. His big brother Chad, doing what his parents had always taught him to do, tried to save him. He, too, fell in. Stevie, strong for his age, also tried to be his brothers' keeper. He broke through the crust.

A neighbor boy ran for help. Frantic firemen pulled the brothers from the pond within 30 minutes. They weren't breathing and had no pulse. Two helicopters and an ambulance took them to three separate hospitals.

So began the agonizing pilgrimage of Charles and Mary Gragg, two ordinary people who now stagger in the footsteps of Job.

Word of the tragedy spread quickly through this western Missouri town of 2,800. The event would change forever Buckner's image of itself.

As doctors at St. Mary's Hospital in nearby Blue Springs told the parents their son Chad was dead, teachers and friends arrived to surround the stunned couple in a protective cocoon.

Hoping against hope, the Graggs next went to St. Luke's Hospital in Kansas City, only to be told Aaron, too, was gone.

By the time they reached Children's Mercy Hospital, the Graggs were at the heart of a caravan of grief. They found Stephen on a life support system. At 10 p.m., he died.

In the space and time it took for the sun to set and the moon to rise, three healthy, happy, handsome little boys vanished from the lives of all who knew them.

They left behind bits of homework and smiling celluloid images, a puppy named Scooter who looks for them everywhere, empty school desks, classmates who struggle to remember their last words, teachers who wish they'd known them better.

They left behind the townspeople of Buckner, who were moved by the loss to dig deep within their hearts and pockets to bury the children with dignity, and continue to mourn them with honest tears.

They left behind their mother and their father, but Mary and Charles Gragg, both 41, are no longer parents. The sounds of laughter, of life, are gone from their house. The only noise comes from the television set. The door to the boys' bedroom is closed.

The unbearable must now be borne.

"In our age, children aren't eligible to die because our expectations have been set up that children can survive anything," said Kathryn Howard, a grief counselor with Comprehensive Mental Health Services in nearby Independence, Mo.

"All the time we read about children who fall into freezing water and survive. Why not Aaron, or Chad, or at least Stevie? They couldn't be saved because the water wasn't deep enough nor cold enough. But because of modern medical miracles, we are conditioned to believe it is outrageous that they died." She added:

"This is now a community that speaks with one voice. That phenomenon is rare—too often we are too big and fragmented a society for this to happen. But if you listen to Buckner today, what you hear is, 'We care. This matters to us. They were our children, too.' "

The Graggs had no close relatives living nearby. Acting out of instinct and compassion, Buckner Elementary School Principal Richard Thompson stepped into the void.

"The school in a sense became their family," said Thompson. "Working with me, Kathryn Howard, and Jerry Brown, the funeral director, Charlie and Mary decided to have the funeral in the junior high gymnasium. The parents wanted the teachers to speak, and to be pallbearers.

"This became a chance for the community to fulfill what a community is all about. Before the accident happened you could have counted on one hand the number of people who knew Charlie and Mary Gragg. Now everyone knows them and wants to help them."

The Parent-Teacher Association mobilized to take food to the Gragg home for the next two weeks. Secretly thanking God it wasn't their own kids, mothers reached into closets and brought forth suits and ties for the boys to wear to their graves.

Funds were established to accept donations to offset medical and funeral expenses. Nearly $20,000 was raised the first two weeks after the accident.

Mortician Brown decided on three identical coffins, three identical hearses. He reserved three side-by-side plots on a gently-sloping hillside in the town cemetery.

From the graves you can look out over the walnut and oak trees, past dormant farm pastures, and down toward the creek where an angry crawdad once bit Aaron's big toe, where Chad caught a two-pound lunker of a catfish, where Stevie loved to hunt for frogs.

As Brown ministered to the dead, Thompson and Ms. Howard, along with every clergyman in town, local teachers, and reinforcements from other schools, consoled the living.

"The day after it happened we conducted emotional triage in the halls, the library, the cafeteria, and the classrooms," said Ms. Howard. "We had kids crying with counselors in corners everywhere you looked. Part of being young is learning how to deal with your pain. The kids were shown they could support one another and that they wouldn't be alone."

Teachers read "The Taste of Blackberries" to all fourth and fifth graders. The book tells of a boy who loses his best friend. Younger children heard "The 10th Good Thing About Barney," a story of a little boy whose cat dies.

Thompson sent letters home with every student, detailing the day's upheaval and warning parents their children "might have tears or depression but that is expected and is normal in the grief process. . . ."

"That day we just put a Band-Aid on it, we flew by the seat of our pants," recalled Thompson. "We decided to leave the Gragg boys' desks empty to stress the finality of death. We talked about the details. We tried to cope with the onslaught of the media but refused to let reporters talk to teachers or students. And we braced for the funeral."

"It was tough trying to make an appropriate setting for a funeral out of a basketball court, but we did it," said Thompson.

He had a carpenter build a little wooden schoolhouse which was then covered with flowers and presented by the students at Buckner. Thompson also gave the parents a brass school bell engraved with the boys' names. The gift usually is reserved for retiring teachers.

"We consider that your boys have retired to a heavenly school," Thompson told the Graggs.

More than 600 mourners heard fourth-grade teacher Jeanne Young describe the Gragg children as "three adventuresome, energetic little boys . . . each of us has a special place in our heart, locked and guarded—it's the place for Chad and Stephen and Aaron."

Symbols of each boy's interests rested atop the blue-gray caskets: art materials for Aaron, a soccer ball for Stephen, a basketball for Chad.

Finally, the three brothers were laid to rest on winter's hard ground.

The Graggs believe they'll stay in the neighborhood where dogs run free and kids' boundaries are defined by a stop sign on a country road.

They speak of their sons in the present tense.

Looking at a small pile of photographs, Mary Gragg remembers each of her sons as a sturdy, blue-eyed, blonde-haired baby.

"They were so good. They slept through the night every night.

"Aaron is my artist, my loner, he loves his dinosaurs. Chad is his daddy made over, my helper, everybody's helper, such a good student. He loves school, he never misses, and he loves riding his bicycle. Stevie's a little slow, a shy kid. Stevie loves Alf. . . ."

Charlie Gragg takes up the sentence.

"You'll never see kids that alike, that close. If one goes out the front door, the other two are right behind. . . . I wasn't surprised they all died trying to pull each other out of that pond.

"I always told them, 'No matter what happens, you help your brothers.' "

Is there anything anyone can do for the Graggs? They say there is nothing. They are baffled that there might be an answer to such a question.

Soon it will be spring, time to go fishin' again, and frog huntin', and crawdad catchin'. That's when the children of Buckner Elementary School will plant three new trees in memory of Aaron, Chad, and Stevie.

By then, the ice will be gone from the ponds.

USAGE: Handling Those Hectoring Hangups

12

Split 'n' Polish

Split infinitives were good enough for William Shakespeare, George Bernard Shaw and a flock of other capable writers. They should be good enough for the rest of us.

Shaw, in fact, once complained to a newspaper about the harrumphings of an anti-splitter.

"Your fatuous specialist," GBS fumed, "is now beginning to rebuke 'second rate' newspapers for using such phrases as 'to suddenly go' and 'to boldly say.' I ask you, sir, to put this man out without interfering with his perfect freedom of choice to suddenly go, to go suddenly, and suddenly to go. Try an intelligent Newfoundland dog in his place."

Split in peace then, but split for good reason: when it sounds better, and when it's to avoid ambiguity.

Some perfectly good splits:

He said he had great difficulty *to really understand* what the government was up to.

Try to put the adverb *really* elsewhere in the sentence without disruption.

137

The cops wanted those youngsters *to really see* the danger.

Painless split, increases emphasis.

They said they would try *to carefully dislodge* the tangle of twisted girders tomorrow.

Smooth enough. *Carefully to dislodge* is impossible, and *to dislodge carefully* doesn't sound right.

On the other hand, there's no point in splitting the infinitive here:

The company hopes *to substantially increase* profits. . . .

increase profits substantially gets the nod. From the ear.

Avoid splitting an infinitive with two or more words:

He said he planned to energetically and devotedly pursue those objectives.

Adverbs after *objectives*, or: . . . *to pursue those objectives with energy and devotion.*

They promised to at all times obey the law of the land.

They promised at all times to obey the law of the land is possible, but . . . *law of the land at all times* seems preferable.

One way to not split an infinitive is with *not, never* or *always,* which go more naturally beforehand:

The mayor asked strikers *to not insist* on the march (*not to insist*).
The president made sure *to always* receive his visitors at the entrance (*always made sure to*).
At the meeting, he advised parents *to never let* the youngsters walk alone (*never to let*).

I hope this is enough to somewhat clear the air.

Genderly Speaking

The point can't be overemphasized: words must fit together naturally, comfortably, so they do not distract the reader by calling attention to themselves. In the effort to rid the language of male bias—a commendable effort—distraction often results. Nowhere is the straining for fairness more contrived than in the juggling of personal pronouns.

> The mayor warned every homeowner that he or she is responsible for clearing the snow in front of his or her house.

The writer didn't want to imply that all homeowners are male, so instead he danced awkwardly around the problem, kicking up clouds of clutter. In this case, and all like it, the solution is easy. Recast the sentence to use the sexually neutral plural pronoun:

> The mayor warned all homeowners that they are responsible for clearing the snow in front of their houses.

The baby who sucks his thumb can as clearly and naturally be written *babies who suck their thumbs. A reporter tries to protect his sources* can, eliminating bias, become *reporters try to protect their sources.*

But what if there is no graceful way around the singular pronoun? Should the sentence two paragraphs back have said *he or she danced awkwardly around the problem,* or, almost as clumsily, repeated *the writer* instead of using the pronoun *he?*

I say no. So does the *AP Stylebook.* Avoid presumptions of maleness whenever possible. Be especially alert for such constructions as *the boss . . . he* which imply that only males are bosses. At the same time, avoid straining for neutrality through constructions that jar and call attention to themselves. Let good judgment tell you whether it is a case of a permissible *he* or a case of presumed maleness that should be avoided.

As for nouns, apply the same rule. When the choice is a natural one—*reporter* for *newsman, firefighter* for *fireman, worker* for *workingman, mail carrier* for *mailman*—use the word that includes both sexes. But avoid manufactured contrivances such as *spokesperson.*

Substitutions: Terminal and Incipient

The old superstition, based on a grammatical fallacy, that no sentence should end with a preposition, is happily dying out. For that matter, most good writers down the ages have ignored it.

Police recovered the bloody ax he killed her with is good English, whereas *Police recovered the bloody ax with which he killed her* is stodgy.

As Winston Churchill said, it's a "pedantry up with which we will not put."

Some traditionalists also cling to another myth: Sentences must not start with *and* or *but*. No reason why they shouldn't, though in practice it's often overdone. Look over the initial *ands* and *buts* you write. And see if they are superfluous, as the *and* is in this sentence.

But implies a contrast, and for that reason—not because of its position—it is wrong here:

The defendant appeared dejected by his wife's outburst. But the prosecutor indicated he might recall her later.

An *and* would be possible, but actually neither is needed.

It's All Relative

Careful writers insist on correct use of the relative pronouns *that* and *which* not merely out of respect for syntax but in the cause of clarity. The two words are used in restrictive and non-restrictive clauses, respectively, and are not interchangeable. The following two sentences do not mean the same thing:

The bicycle that was on the porch was stolen.

The bicycle which was on the porch was stolen.

The first sentence leaves the implication that of several bicycles, the one that was stolen was the one on the porch. The second sentence provides the non-essential fact of the theft that the stolen bicycle happened to be on the porch.

RULE: Use *which* for non-defining, non-limiting clauses; use *that* for clauses that define.

Here is a way to remember. If you could put the clause in parentheses or set it off with commas, use *which*. If the clause is necessary to full understanding, use *that*.

The stream, which [by the way] rises dangerously during the flood season, flows near the village.

The stream that rises dangerously during the flood season [as opposed to other streams] flows near the village.

Legalism

And/or is something that lawyers seem to enjoy and it's one of those happy turns that makes legal forms so attractive.

Leave it to them. It's always avoidable:

The officers thought they would find the loot and/or other evidence at the scene. (Either *and* or *or* but not both.)

The force was to consist of National Guardsmen and/or state police. (National Guardsmen or state police or both.)

Attorneys, in the ritual of avoiding leading questions and/or (chuckle) the appearance of prejudgment, fling themselves at *if any*. Some news writers are impressed by the sound, though it's rarely sensible in copy:

There was a question what effect, if any, the company proposal would have on the rank and file.

Since the proposal was bound to have some effect, omit *if any*. If you want to quibble about that, there is still another way: *If the proposal would have any effect . . .*

Here's a case where a reporter was more lawyerly than the lawyers:

None of the lawyers involved would say what legal strategy, if any, they would take.

Candidates for disbarment, I'd say, if there's a chance that they would not adopt any legal strategy.

Subjunctivitis

Writers sometimes tense up over things that haven't happened, though they have, and flee into the "woulds."

Still, McEnroe did not concede the third set. As he *would* say later, he had opportunities to win throughout the match.

There's nothing incorrect about the subjunctive construction, but why not make it *as he said afterward?*
The *woulds* thicken menacingly in this lead:

MEXIA, Texas—The party would go on all night. But at 11 p.m., as the festivities were just gathering steam, the drownings that would mar memories of the day and create a furor whose tremors would reach Washington were about to happen.

That lead creates an eerie backward-forward-not yet effect, and it isn't helped by the dreadful gulf between *drownings* and *were about to happen.*
The following gets us out of the time warp:

MEXIA, Texas—The party went on all night and was just gathering steam when the drownings occurred. Later, the tragedy marred the memories of the day and raised a furor whose tremors reached Washington.

If the extended subjunctive seems a clumsy way to grapple with the future, the fatuous backward glance seems even worse. This makes much too much of the fact that the future is unknowable:

Little did Joe Smith know, when he peered shortsightedly at the blackboard in first grade, that he would some day be Smithtown's leading ophthalmologist.

That is a hypothetical example, but representative. Here is an actual example from a newspaper:

When Sidney Sheldon was writing his latest best seller, he probably had no idea it would be used as a challenge by those who have been saying that the Washington County library in Abingdon is loaded with dirty books.

The absurdity is compounded by the cautious *probably.*

You would do well to avoid the subjunctive if you can, and to leave speculative flashbacks alone altogether.

Dash It All

A lot of writers like to toss around dashes to keep things stirred up. They look, well, more dashing than the crooked little comma, the hangdog semicolon and the obese parenthesis, for all of which dashes are frequently misused.

The comma indicates a slight break in the thought of a sentence; the semicolon a rather larger one, and the dash an abrupt, dramatic turn. Dashes, therefore, should be used sparingly; overuse weakens their effect. They often add a jarring note to an otherwise smooth sentence.

The dash is used correctly here:

They trudged wearily along the trail—dozens had died on it, and they knew it—until they made camp utterly exhausted.

But not in the following examples:

He said his grandmother— who had just reached 93—was a "very vigorous old lady."

No abrupt break in the thought. Commas instead of dashes.

The defendant said he hadn't known she had left—without explanation.

Fake dramatics. . . . *had left without explanation.*

The 4,372-piece set—an average $48 per piece—had arrived at the White House by truck from the Lenox China plant . . .

Parentheses or commas.

Their arrival meant that suburbia—which has sprawled slowly across North Jersey since the 1930s—had finally pierced the state's westernmost farming country.

Commas.

The burden of clerical rule—including the banning of alcoholic beverages, Western music and movies; requirements that women be veiled, and Islamic punishments, including death for what are deemed sexual offenses—has fallen most heavily on the Westernized, the educated, and the middle class.

The dash must have looked to the writer as the only way to save this sentence. Had he tried parentheses or commas, he might have realized that he needed to go back to the drawing board.

Lay On, MacDuff

Despite the twanging testimony of country singers, it is possible to use *lie* and *lay* correctly.

I suspect the confusion stems from the fact that *to lay*, meaning "to place something on a surface," is also the past tense of *to lie*, meaning "to recline." To make matters worse, *to lie* is also the verb that means "to tell a falsehood," an inflammatory word that may cause some to flinch and use *lay*, incorrectly, in its place.

Lay aside, for a moment, the falsehood meaning of *lie* and concentrate on the two verbs that are so often confused. Start with the principal parts:

Verb 1—lie, lay, lain.

Verb 2—lay, laid, laid.

The derelict stumbled to the park to *lie* on a bench. He selected the same bench that he *lay* on yesterday. He has *lain* on the same bench every night for the past week.

He looked for a place to *lay* his knapsack. He *laid* it beside the bench in the same place as yesterday, the same place he has *laid* it for a week.

Remember: *to lay* takes an object; *to lie* does not.

Et Cetera

At the end of a sentence containing a string of words or phrases separated by commas, writers sometimes feel compelled to attach a meaningless little tail designed to tell the reader, "This is an incomplete list."

The adult education program offers a wide variety of courses, such as woodworking, French cookery, creative writing and origami, *among others*.

He stays active during his leisure hours with golf, carpentry, birdwatching, fishing, hiking *and similar activities*.

There's a way out of that hangup. In the first example, delete the *and* before the final item on the list and insert a comma: . . . *cooking, creative writing, origami.* In the second example, just cross out *and similar activities.*

The simple trick of omitting *and* before the final item in a list suggests it is an incomplete list. Read it aloud and you will see.

Numbers Game

Numbers go into stories for precision. The way they're often handled, though, makes them sorry figures—vague and confusing enough to have readers muttering to themselves.

Let us count the ways:

1. The More-Less Seesaw

Johnson got *more* than $100,000 *less* than he expected.

First, try to get an exact figure. (We hide too often behind approximations.) Failing, write it this way: *Johnson expected at least $100,000 more than he got.*

Fewer than the more than 60,000 ticketholders showed up.

At least 60,000 bought tickets, but not all of them showed up.

The staff of the state Utilities Commission recommended a $4.7 million rate hike for Carolina Telephone & Telegraph Co. But the recommended figure is *more than* $21 million *less than* the company expected.

I suspect one more phone call would have gotten the reporter the exact sum. Otherwise, *at least* is again the way out.

2. Mathematical Leads

A jury of four men and eight women deliberated more than 21 hours before convicting a 19-year-old high school dropout of killing his 18-year-old girlfriend two years ago.

Too much. Stats-happy sportswriters also are prone to throw these curve balls:

The rangy, 6-foot-6 forward who just turned 20 scored 22 points to Tibbets' 18 as the Jays pulled out the game with eight seconds to go for their 10th straight victory. They had trailed 34-33 at halftime.

KANSAS CITY, Mo.—Nick Lowery kicked field goals of 20, 20, 42 and 41 yards Sunday, leading Kansas City . . .

3. Bottomless Pit.

The company's losses could total up to $11 million . . .

Or as little as $2.50? Try to give the range: *Could lose from $6 million to $11 million.*

4. Math Test

When they first met, Klipstein was nearly twice the younger man's age.

And how much was that? Klipstein's age was given five grafs earlier. The younger man's age was never given.

This was about two-thirds the amount they spent for food.

This story made the reader backtrack four grafs to find the food budget, then figure the two-thirds.

5. Execrable Approximations

About, almost and other fudges are sometimes necessary (don't write *approximately* or *some*) but they're best used with round figures only.

About 112 policemen were sent to the scene of the disturbance.

Again, the best solution is *at least.*

More than 13 people were in the group, and police seized *some* three.

The reader wonders why the reporter couldn't have gotten such a low count right. Otherwise, fall back on *at least.*

And don't say *about* when the number is exact and should be ascertained for the story: ". . . who handles newsprint purchases for the Gannett group of *about* 80 newspapers." No. Use the exact number. To do otherwise is just lazy.

6. Do the Arithmetic

When editing a story with numbers in it, double-check the writer's arithmetic. If the story enumerates groups of various sizes, for example, make sure the numbers total the figure in the lead. In short, do the math.

That's That

Some sentences read well without *that*, others don't. There's no rule about when to put it in. It is true, though, that you can never go wrong by including it, while you can cause small disturbances by omitting it.

No problem with the absence of *that* in these sentences:

The commissioner said she was sure they would comply.

The secretary disclosed he would leave for Paris tomorrow.

There's something wrong with the following, however:

Mayor Koch said years ago, the city had tried this method of financing but had failed.

That reads at first blush as though the mayor had said it years ago. *That* after *said* would have been better.

He said in a survey of state motels by the state association, it was discovered . . .

Again, *that* after said. He didn't say it in a survey.

You must always use *that* when the word following a verb may be wrongly construed as its object:

The teacher reported the children who threw the books would be disciplined.

The committee vote signaled the bill stands a good chance of passing.

Without *that* after *reported* in the first example and *signaled* in the second, you have the teacher reporting the children and the vote signaling the bill. The reader is momentarily misled. Insert *that* after the verb to keep the meaning clear and the writing smooth.

It's usually better to use *that* when a time element comes between the verb and the *that* clause:

The agency said today it will have additional shipments en route.

Slightly awkward, and the *today* may be briefly taken to refer to the shipments.

Stephens said he would like to seek a compromise with Williams before taking the bill up in his committee because he believes the

House of Delegates would approve the bill as before, but it is of little value if it is destined to die in the Senate.

This seems to require a *that* after the *but,* since the clause otherwise reads like the reporter's comment. A *that* in this second clause would also call for a *that* after *said.* A *but that* or *and that* in the second clause needs a parallel *that* in the first.

What's in It for Me?

Science writers and others on specialty beats know that part of their job is to translate—to reduce the vocabulary of, say, genetic engineering to lay terms. Covering legislatures and government usually doesn't entail such mysteries, but there are other hangups. Jargon, dealt with elsewhere, is one. So is an obsession with mechanics.

A common pitfall for legislative reporters is the notion that readers share the insider's passion for procedural detail and political shadow boxing. What readers want to know, right off the bat, is what's in it for them—the practical consequences. Legislative coverage and other governmental reporting that loses sight of this is writing tailored to the reporter's pressroom pals, cloakroom pols and agency moles.

Note how blurry the one point of reader interest becomes under inconsequential mechanics:

BOSTON—The Massachusetts Legislature has finalized action on a bill providing for a public vote in the November election on the question of repealing the state's Sunday closing laws.

By a voice vote, the Senate enacted the bill Monday and sent it to the governor.

The last obstacle to the enactment of the bill was removed when the House, on a 178-33 roll call, voted not to reconsider its enactment of the passed the bill several weeks ago.

BOSTON—The Massachusetts Legislature has decided to give voters a chance to say whether they want the state's blue laws repealed.

Under those ancient statutes, dating to colonial days, most businesses must be closed on Sunday.

The voters' verdict in November will not be binding on the Legislature. Business generally favors repeal, while some unions oppose it.

| The measure provides for a non-binding referendum on the blue laws, which require that most business activity cease on Sunday. | The Sentate passed the bill setting up the referendum and sent it to the governor Monday. A move to block the measure in the House failed. |

The right-hand version focuses on the substance of the legislation, while the original emphasizes procedure at needless length.

BISMARCK, N.D.—The 44th Legislative Assembly convenes Tuesday for the opening of what most legislative leaders have called one of the most important sessions in the state's history.

Few care what legislative leaders call it. More to the point was material that didn't come up until the fourth paragraph:

BISMARCK, N.D.—The Legislative Assembly opening Tuesday will have to deal with the largest budget in North Dakota history and grapple with decisions about coal development in the western part of the state.

The following was intended mainly as a human (or animal) interest story. Why encumber the lead with legislative detail?

| WASHINGTON — Members of a House-Senate conference committee agreed today on a legislative package for western ranges that includes provisions for giving away wild horses and burros to anyone willing to care for the animals. | WASHINGTON—If you want a wild horse or a burro, just promise you'll take good care of it and it's yours, courtesy of Congress. |

In short, don't put the cart before the burro.

BESTIARY
A Compendium
for the Careful
and the
Crotchety

13

Standards of written English are not rigid. Some usages blossom briefly and die; others take root and enrich the language. The process is slow and unpredictable. Meanwhile, careful users of the language often disagree on this or that locution.

That said, what follows here is a collection of usages that I regard as bestial. (In the matter of misuse of words, I allow myself to overstate.) Some of the entries, at this stage in the development of the language, allow for no argument. If you write *disinterested* when you mean *uninterested* you are wrong, period. Other entries, I admit, may be open to discussion—but not if I'm handling the copy. Every editor has crotchets. Among these are some of mine.

A BEFORE H.   Unless you're prepared to write *an* horse, *an* ham, or *an* hamburger, make it *a* historian, *a* historical or *a* hysterical moment. The initial *H* in those words is pronounced, or rather aspirated, unlike in *hour* or *honest*, which take *an*.

ACTIVE CONSIDERATION.   Have you ever heard of anybody giving a plan or proposal passive consideration? This is bureaucratic baloney meant to sound grander than *thinking it over.*

AD HOC.   In Latin, it means "toward this." An *ad hoc* committee is one appointed to deal with one particular case or problem. Officialdom loves to go off ad hocked, and so does the business world. But why? If you write, *The league appointed a committee to oversee the flower show*, the *ad hoc* is understood. Or you could say, *a special committee.* Use something other than *ad hoc*—at least *pro tem.*

ADDRESS.   A favorite pomposity of academia now spread like a fungus. *Address* a letter. Don't address a problem. Instead, deal with it, take it up, consider it, tackle it, cope with it.

ALTERNATELY/ALTERNATIVELY.   Don't confuse the two. The first means "by turns": *They traveled alternately by snowmobile and dogsled.* If only one were available, they would go by dog sled, or, *alternatively*, by snowmobile.

AMBIVALENT.   This word is sometimes misused for *ambiguous. Ambivalent*, a term from psychoanalysis, means that two irreconcilable emotions are operating in the mind (love-hate, for example). *Mixed feelings* is a less pretentious substitute. *Ambiguous* is applied only to written or spoken statements and means "having several possible meanings": *The employer was ambivalent about the applicant because of his ambiguous answers.*

ANTIQUE.   The trouble with *antique* is that it is both a noun and an adjective. An antique is a rare old object. An antique clock is a rare old clock. If you want to describe a rare old store you could conceivably call it an antique store. But if you mean a store that trades in rare old objects, it is an *antiques* store. A person who deals in *antique* objects is an *antiques* dealer.

ANYMORE.   When the *Webster III* dictionary came out, language purists were shocked that it permitted *any more* to be written as one word, *anymore.* Well, all right (NEVER *alright*), I don't like it a lot (NEVER *alot*), but will go along—with this reservation: When you're writing about something additional, make it two words: *I don't want any more advice from you.* When it's used as an adverb, as in, *I don't want to argue with that editor any-*

more, go ahead and make it one word. By the way, if you've ever written *some place* as one word, don't do it any more.

CHARISMA. Properly a theological term for the special grace that gives saints their power; a divine gift. For lesser mortals, *appeal, magnetism, attractiveness*, are all more appropriate. Nowadays, *charisma* is used for any ward politican with a smooth voice and a knack for getting votes.

COMMUNITY. For some reason, perhaps because the bonds that make up a true community are scarce and getting scarcer, the noun is applied these days to professions, occupations and virtually any conglomeration of people sharing peripheral interests. So we see *medical community, engineering community, business community* and may soon see *trash collectors' community*. Write *doctors, engineers, business (people)* and, by all means, *trash collectors*.

CONCEPT. Pompous noun for *idea, notion, scheme*. Use one of those less grand words unless you're referring to something complex, like Einstein's concept of the universe, or Kung's concept of the church. Not *the mayor's new concept of parking lot use*. (Be careful of *notion*, though. It's often used as a sneer word, meaning a sort of harebrained idea: *He had a notion he could halt the arms race*.)

CONCEPTUALIZE. Same thing. Fit for, say, an effort to conceptualize the movement of subatomic particles. But why bother? What's wrong with *envision*?

CONFRONTATION. An all-purpose word from the seething Sixties that has long since turned mushy. When possible, reach for the specifics: *noisy argument, shoving match, scuffle, exchange of insults, ultimatum*.

CONVINCE, PERSUADE. *Convince* requires a state of mind, *persuade* a course of action. A person often acts in accordance with convictions, but not necessarily. The editor may try to convince you that a lead is poor; failing, he may persuade you to change it anyway. The distinction is valuable and should be preserved. Think: convince *that*, persuade *to*.

DICHOTOMY.   It means "a split or division into two contradictory or mutually exclusive parts": truth and falsehood, right and wrong. *Split* or *division* are always preferable in news writing.

DILEMMA.   If we restrict this word (or any word) to its precise meaning we keep its usefulness. *Dilemma* is not a synonym of *predicament* or *jam* or *trouble*. It means that someone faces two alternative courses of action, both of which are likely to be unpleasant. "On the horns of a dilemma" is a cliché to be avoided, but it does illustrate the special problem the word defines.

DISINTERESTED.   Does not mean *un*interested. *Dis*interested means personally detached, unbiased in a matter in which you have no stake. *Un*interested simply means lacking interest. You can be *dis*interested in your friend's divorce without being at all *un*interested. As a reporter you should always be *dis*interested but never *un*interested.

EXCELLENCE, PURSUIT OF.   Shopworn to the point anything associated with excellence should never be. A favored, if immodest, characterization by certain professional groups of their current scrambling. Sometimes unavoidable in direct quotes; use with extreme caution at other times.

EXPECT/ANTICIPATE.   Politicians and others given to pretentiousness often substitute *anticipate* for *expect*. The words do not mean the same and the distinction should be kept. To *expect* is simply "to look ahead to." *Citrus growers* expect *about the same production as last year*. The word *anticipate* means "to look ahead to—and do something about it." *They put smudge pots in the groves,* anticipating *frost*.

EXPLICATE.   If you like *replicate*, you'll love *explicate*, a pompous word for *explain*. Literary critics embrace it to sound important: *Nowhere is Mr. Thomas's exegesis more clearly explicated* . . . Extricate me!

FARTHER/FURTHER.   Correct usage requires *farther* when speaking of literal distance; *further* in all other instances. *My desk is* farther *from the water cooler than yours. Your daughter is* further *along in school than mine.* But be careful. The expression *taking it a step* further, for example, is correct because *step* is used metaphorically, not as a literal measure of distance.

FEWER/LESS.   That beer does not have *less* calories, that beer has *fewer* calories. *Less* applies to quantities, *fewer* to numbers. Ironclad rule: *less* modifies a singular noun, *fewer* modifies a plural noun. *Fewer* calories, *less* taste.

FLAUNT/FLOUT.   A TV announcer reported, "Doctors with MD plates sometimes flaunt the law." *Flaunt* means "boastfully exhibiting." If you've got it, flaunt it. *Flout* means "defy." What the doctors did with the MD plates was flout the law and flaunt their profession.

FORTUNATE/FORTUITOUS.   Although some, seeking pomposity, substitute *fortuitous* for *fortunate*, the words are not synonymous. *Fortunate* means "lucky." *Fortuitous* means "by chance," "by accident." Something which is *fortuitous* can also be *fortunate*, but unless it happened by chance, *fortunate* is the correct word: *It was <u>fortunate</u> that the plane had enough fuel to reach an alternate landing field. The pilot's choice was <u>fortuitous</u>; all the other fields were damaged.*

FOUNDER/FLOUNDER.   *Without steam, the pumps could not function and the ship began to flounder and go down.* No, it didn't. It began to *founder*, that is "to collapse, to break down suddenly." To *flounder* means "to move clumsily, awkwardly, in confusion"—probably a blend of *founder* and *blunder*. (When that foundering ship sank, a flounder [noun] might have watched.)

FROM . . . TO.   This construction denotes a logical progression, as from A to Z or from girlhood to womanhood, or from stock room to board room, or from soup to nuts. To write *activities that range from golf to investing* begs the question; what goes between? To write *from golf to investing to racing to poker* is worse. What you probably mean is, *as diverse as*. If so, say so.

FULSOME.   It does not mean "lavish" or "bountiful," as in *fulsome praise*. It means "revolting, noisome." The word is now so often misused that a lot of people will misunderstand when you use it correctly. The literate, who are also part of the readership, will applaud. This does, however, raise the point of *fulsome*'s usefulness. There are plenty of substitutes.

HOPEFUL/FEARFUL.   They were fearful that he might be ill, and hopeful that he would recover. A $10,000 reward for proof that these words improve upon, *They were grateful that he had returned, feared he might be ill, and hoped he would recover.* (The battle against *hopefully*, used in the sense of "we hope" [*Hopefully the Dodgers will win the pennant.*] seems hopeless— hopefulless?—but fight on.) These formulations have already betrayed at least one writer into *she said shamefully*, when she meant *shamefacedly*. For shame.

INFER/IMPLY.   *The official complained that the newspaper story falsely inferred that he had condoned racial hatred.* The word the writer intended was *implied*. *Infer* means "to deduce or judge from evidence." *Imply* means "to intimate, to signify, to hint."

INNOVATIVE.   Ridden hard by advertising copywriters and institutional and political boasters and propagandists, this adjective is nearly exhausted. Few programs, policies or people are truly original. Reserve the word for such rare instances. Renaming three courses in its curriculum doesn't make Podunk College an *innovative* school.

INPUT.   Nice computer term, so let's keep it in the technical kennel. In human affairs, warm-blooded words are better: *They sought a stronger voice, or a greater say, at city hall, not more input.*

INTERFACE.   A technical word from science and engineering that jargoneers find irresistible. It means a connection between independent systems, as between a computer and a typesetting machine. Showoffs apply it to human relations, where *coordination, agreement, something in common, shared,* are all better terms. *Doctors and nurses should interface more in a hospital setting* might be tough if many wear glasses. Why not work together? Do we interface on this point?

KUDOS.   The Greeks had a word for it and it was *kydos*, meaning "glory." It has come to us almost intact as *kudos*, meaning "acclaim in recognition of achievement." It is a good word to avoid because it often sounds wrong when used correctly, as in *kudos is in order for Joe Smith*. It is a singular noun in the same way that *pathos*, of similar Greek origin, is singular. There is no such word as *kudo* just as there is no such word as *patho*. If you simply avoid *kudos* it will be to your glory.

LEGENDARY.   Crops up now and then in the hype mode: *Johnny Bench, the legendary catcher*. He's nothing of the sort. A legend is a story handed down from earlier times that's widely believed to be true; the legend of the headless horseman, for example. It's still a myth, though, which Johnny Bench isn't. The epithet was applied by a headless writer.

LIFESTYLE.   Overworked vogue word, usually just a flossy way of saying *life* or *way of living*. *After years of comfort and luxury, financial setbacks changed his lifestyle (life). Some Acapulcans have a splendid lifestyle (live splendidly)*. It is time for this trendy locution to die, in style.

LITERALLY.   Disastrous as a casual intensifier because it means that something is factually and precisely true. *The Mets literally slaughtered the Cardinals last night* would have left at least nine corpses. I would never use *literally* in a million years. I mean that figuratively.

MEDIA.   This word is plural. The press is a news *medium*, television is a *medium*, radio is a *medium*. Together they are news *media*. Never write, *The media is sometimes guilty of bad grammar*. Write, *The media are . . .*

MILITATE/MITIGATE.   The words are confusing because they sound and look alike. They aren't the least similar in meaning. *Militate* (from the Latin word for soldier) means "to have weight or effect." *Mitigate* (from the Latin "to soften") means just that: "to soften, make less severe or painful, alleviate, mollify." *The judge mitigated the sentence from 30 days to 10. The unpredictable economy militates against long-term planning.* Choose plainer words.

NAVAL.   This maritime adjective sometimes comes out *navel*, always good for a belly laugh. The variety of orange, though, is correctly *navel*, because that's what that scar resembles where it was attached, umbilically, to a blossom.

NOTION.   See CONCEPT.

NOUNS INTO VERBS.   Turning nouns into verbs has a long and honorable tradition: *to telephone, to cable*, and the more recent *to bus*. *To contact* is borderline usage, handy only when the nature of the contact is nebulous: letter, telephone call, native runner? But draw the line at noun-spawned verbs that serve no real need and sound gushy, like *debut, host, author*. People *make their debuts, give parties, write books*. Especially execrable is *debut* in the past tense: *The new edition debuted three months ago*.

OBJECTIVE.   No one important likes to have a mere *aim* or *goal*, but an objective. In most uses, *aim* or *goal* is better.

ONLY.   Be careful where you place this trouble-fraught little modifier. Put *only* before any word in the following seven-word sentence and you get seven different meanings: *I hit him in the eye yesterday*. But don't get pedantic about it. In such commonly understood phrases as *I only want orange juice*, placement of *only* where it strictly belongs (before *orange juice*) seems stilted. I'm only trying to help.

OPTION.   If you don't like this word, which bureaucrats and academic babblers have made *de rigueur*, you have an option: *choice*. Same with the verb *opt*: choose *choose*.

PERCEIVE.   Blown-up word for *see, understand, grasp, realize*, spewn into the conversational mainstream via academia. Through overuse for the sake of perceptual elegance, also becoming a weasel word, beclouding the obvious. *Jamaica's economic decline under Prime Minister Manley was perceived as a major cause of his defeat*. Perceived, because it was. Omit *perceived as*.

PLUS.   Advertisers kidnapped this innocent word from mathematicians as a trendy replacement for *also*, or *moreover* or *not only that, but*, none of which needs replacing. Let us restore *plus* to the mathematicians. Minus, never start a sentence with it.

PRAGMATIC.   Imported from philosophy, where it means the intellectual acceptance of whatever is workable as "true," or at least sound. A pragmatist may dislike phonics in principle, but accept it as a workable way to teach reading. But if somebody knows how to deal with insurance salesmen, bank statements and a leaky faucet, he's not pragmatic, he's practical.

PRE-DAWN DARKNESS.   Hackneyed journalese. Write *pre-dawn darkness* if you're also prepared to write *pre-dusk brightness*. It is a poetic phrase that has been worked to death, that's all. A substitute is needed. How about *ere Aurora arose*? No? Then let us return, simply, to *before dawn*.

PRESTIGIOUS.   This, along with *coveted*, is an automatic modifier that pops up drearily with *award, trophy, honor*. You even see the *prestigious Nobel Prize* and the *coveted Pulitzer Prize*. It goes without saying, so don't say it.

REASON WHY.   When *reason* is used as a noun, try never to follow it with *why*. The reason I urge this (not the *reason why* I urge this) is to reduce clutter. *Why* after *reason* is almost always superfluous. When the tone is conversational, though, it's sometimes hard to avoid the *why*—but I see no reason why rules should not have exceptions, do you?

REFER.   *Refer back* is tautological; it's the only way to go. Same is true of *revert back*. That *re* prefix means back. Redundant.

REFUTE/REBUT.   A subtle distinction here, but important, especially in journalism, to avoid editorializing unwittingly. *Refute* renders a verdict; it means "to disprove, to demolish an argument." *Rebut* means "to answer charges or allegations by counterargument." Even though most dictionaries give *rebut* the secondary meaning of "disprove," the word isn't safe. *Reply to, contend, contradict* are neutral substitutes for *rebut* and probably better than *refute*.

RELATE TO.   A vogue term, probably from the social sciences, with a dogged power of endurance. Its vagueness masks any interesting specifics of the relationship. If little Mary fails to *relate to* her peers, she may be a bully, she may be shy, or she may limp. For these or other reasons, she can't seem to make friends. That's a human way of putting it.

REPLICATE.   Scientists like to use *replicate* instead of *repeat exactly*, or *duplicate*. Let 'em.

SCENARIO.   Tom Barber, word-watcher at the *Milwaukee Journal*, calls it "one of those tiresome Watergate words, coined by a bunch of generals, probably, as they plotted deploying their deterrent firepower to neutralize an aggressor." Amen. Barber made a list of 99 alternate words. He wasn't even breathing hard.

SELF-CONFESSED.   Until you discover a way for someone to confess in another person's behalf, write *confessed*.

SKILLS.   Pedagogues' padding. *Mastering mathematical skills, teaching reading skills*. Make it *mastering mathematics, teaching to read*.

SOPHISTICATED.   A cliché adjective that writers apply to any piece of technology that's over their heads. Computers, as a class, for example, are no longer so remarkable that they need to be tagged as sophisticated. Neither are F-16s. Because so much is, in comparison with the ordinary writer's mechanical aptitude, sophisticated, the adjective should be used sparingly.

SPELLING.   The English language embraces so many variations in spelling that some words, like the multiplication tables, just have to be memorized. Start with these 20 and add your own: *accommodate, affidavit, asinine, consensus, diphtheria, embarrass, harass, imposter, impresario, inoculate, liquefy, pavilion, precede, rarefy, resuscitate, rococo, sacrilegious, siege, supersede, titillate*.

STANCE.   Means primarily a standing position, as a fighter or golfer might take. Now it is used for *attitude, position, philosophy: his foreign policy stance*. There's nothing drastically wrong with it except that it's becoming worn out, like *posture*.

STRATEGY.   Bow-wow language. Use *plan, scheme, design, method. The housing agency has several strategies for dealing with urban poverty* sounds important in a handout, which is why it's there. Make it *has several ways of dealing with poverty*. Academics, of course, talk about *new strategies in curricular reform*, but there is no redeeming them.

SUBSUME.   As soon as academics began sprinkling their learned papers with this vogue word, bureaucrats jumped all over it. Most of them misuse it. *Subsume* means "to include within a larger group." *The question of twice-weekly garbage pickup was subsumed by the debate over the whole municipal budget*. Probably because it looks and sounds like *consume*, some mistakenly take it to mean "to eat up." Don't you.

SUPPORTIVE OF.   Why weaken a decent verb by turning it into an adjective with a preposition? *He was supportive of the fund drive?* What mush. *He supported the fund drive.*

SURROGATE.   Hard to know, or judge, how this word invaded political babble, as in *the president's surrogates. Representatives, stand-ins, substitutes* are better words, although politicians will prefer the more imposing one.

TENSIONS, RELAXATION OF.   Staple of diplomatic language, where vagueness is often useful. Overblown when used for more mundane affairs, such as a school board squabbling with teachers, a baseball manager at odds with the owner. (Is it a *détente* if they become friendly again?) *The fact that contract negotiations with the meat packers resumed signaled a relaxation of tensions.* Make it *brightened hopes for a settlement,* or some such.

THRUST.   Doesn't blast off quite as frequently as it used to, but it's still tired and, by association with the types who keep using it as a noun, pompous. *The thrust of the 21-page report. . .* Make it *gist, tenor, drift, burden.*

UTILIZE.   No discernible reason why anyone would want to substitute that verb for *use.* They have exactly the same meaning, so why choose the longer and ugly word over the short and crisp one? Use *use.*

VERBAL/ORAL.   *Verbal* applies to any use of language, either spoken or written. *Oral* applies to spoken language only. *He made a verbal commitment* is nonsense.

VIABLE.   In its original sense in the life sciences, *viable* means "capable of survival and growth." Now it is used for *real, workable, practical, sound, healthy.* If those splendid words needed technical reinforcement, *viable* would be all right. But there is no need for it, and, besides, misuse robs *viable* of a limited and precise meaning.

VIABLE ALTERNATIVE.   Used in *viable's* (regrettably) expanded sense to mean "a sound or workable alternative." But does anyone ever seek an unsound or unworkable alternative? The adjective is redundant; leave it out. The same often applies to modifiers for *solution* and *option*.*

VIRTUAL.   It doesn't mean "actual," and it doesn't mean "nearly," either. *Virtual* means that something has the effect but not the form. *When the president resigned, the vice president became the <u>virtual</u> head of the company* (even though he had not been so named).

WHENCE, ALBEIT, WHEREIN, THUS.   All somewhat archaic and therefore (not *hence*) undesirable. But if you must use *whence*, it means "from where"; *from whence* is tautological.

WORKAHOLIC.   This was a bright coinage back when it identified a person truly addicted to work. Now it has been reduced to describing anyone who stays late at the office. Time to put it aside to dry out—along with all the other *aholics: cleanaholic* (tidy housekeeper), *runaholic* (jogger), and, so help me, *wordaholic* (scrupulous editor). I need a drink.

YOUTH.   A respectable noun that few ever use in conversation. You talk about *children, adolescents, teen-agers, young people, the youth of America,* perhaps, but can you hear yourself saying, *Suzie next door is an interesting youth*? No? Then think twice before you use the word in copy.

---

*The (Toronto) *Globe and Mail* quoted a doctor who carried the locution to the absurd: "If someone is confronted with certain knowledge that he or she is going to die a painful death through terminal illness, then suicide can be a viable option."

 **BOOKS**

FOR COLLEGE AND BEYOND

Test Preparation

Cram Course for the GMAT
Cram Course for the GRE
Cram Course for the LSAT
Cram Course for the MAT
Getting Into Law School
Getting Into Medical School
GMAT: Graduate Management Admission Test
GRE: Graduate Record Examination, General Test
GRE • GMAT Math Review
GRE in Biology
GRE in Computer Science
GRE in Engineering
GRE in Psychology
GRE • LSAT Logic Workbook
LSAT: Law School Admission Test
MAT: Miller Analogies Test
MCAT Sample Exams
MCAT Science Review
Nursing School Entrance Examinations
PCAT: Pharmacy College Admission Test
Scoring High on Bar Exam Essays
SuperCourse for the GMAT
SuperCourse for the GRE
SuperCourse for the LSAT
SuperCourse for the MCAT

Study Aids

How to Develop and Write a Research Paper
How to Read and Interpret Poetry
How to Read and Write About Fiction
How to Write About Drama
How to Write Book Reports
How to Write Poetry
How to Write Themes and Essays
How to Write a Thesis
Sourcebook for English Papers
Webster's New World™ Student Writing Handbook
10,000 Ideas for Term Papers, Projects, Reports, and Speeches

Professional Certification and Licensing

The AICPA's Uniform CPA Exam Review, 1992 Edition
Math Review for Real Estate License Examinations
Mutual Funds and Annuities Exam
National Commodity Futures Exam
NTE: National Teacher's Exam
PPST: Pre-Professional Skills Test
Real Estate License Examinations
Registered Representative / Stockbroker Exam
SuperCourse for Real Estate Licensing
Teacher Certification Tests
Uniform Securities Agent State Law Exam

Career Reference

The Complete Resume Guide
Federal Jobs for College Graduates
Federal Jobs in Law Enforcement
How to Pass Clerical Employment Tests
How to Pass Employment Tests
How You Really Get Hired
Make Your Job Interview a Success
Passport to Overseas Employment
Resumes for Better Jobs
Resumes that Get Jobs
Your Resume: Key to a Better Job
250 Home-Based Jobs

General Interest

Blue Pages U.S.A.
Get the Facts on Anyone
How to Pass Employment Tests
Test Your Cultural Literacy
Test Your 80's Cultural Literacy
Test Your I.Q.
What Do You Know About Sex?

AVAILABLE AT BOOKSTORES EVERYWHERE

PRENTICE HALL